What is Ethics?

T0056366

Polity's *What is Philosophy?* series

Sparkling introductions to the key topics
in philosophy, written with zero jargon by
leading philosophers.

Stephen Hetherington, *What is Epistemology?*

James P. Sterba, *What is Ethics?*

Charles Taliaferro, *What is Philosophy
of Religion?*

What is Ethics?

James P. Sterba

polity

First published in 2020 by Polity Press

Polity Press
65 Bridge Street
Cambridge CB2 1UR, UK

Polity Press
101 Station Landing
Suite 300
Medford, MA 02155, USA

ISBN-13: 978-1-5095-3101-1
ISBN-13: 978-1-5095-3102-8 (pb)

A catalogue record for this book is available from the British Library.

Library of Congress Cataloging-in-Publication Data

Names: Sterba, James P., author.
Title: What is ethics? / James P. Sterba.
Description: Medford, MA : Polity, 2019. | Series: What is philosophy? | Includes bibliographical references.
Identifiers: LCCN 2019020139 (print) | LCCN 2019981528 (ebook) | ISBN 9781509531011 (hardback) | ISBN 9781509531028 (pbk.) | ISBN 9781509531042 (ebook)
Subjects: LCSH: Ethics.
Classification: LCC BJ1012 .S693 2019 (print) | LCC BJ1012 (ebook) | DDC 170--dc23
LC record available at https://lccn.loc.gov/2019020139
LC ebook record available at https://lccn.loc.gov/2019981070
Typeset in 11 on 13 pt Sabon by
Servis Filmsetting Ltd, Stockport, Cheshire
Printed and bound in Great Britain by CPI Group (UK) Ltd, Croydon

The publisher has used its best endeavours to ensure that the URLs for external websites referred to in this book are correct and active at the time of going to press. However, the publisher has no responsibility for the websites and can make no guarantee that a site will remain live or that the content is or will remain appropriate.

Every effort has been made to trace all copyright holders, but if any have been overlooked the publisher will be pleased to include any necessary credits in any subsequent reprint or edition.

For further information on Polity, visit our website: politybooks.com

Contents

Author's Note		vi
Acknowledgments		vii
1	Introduction	1
2	Why be Moral?	21
3	Consequentialism	38
4	Nonconsequentialism	53
5	Reconciliation	71
6	Morality and Religion	92
7	Conclusion	108
Notes		118
Selected Bibliography		130

Author's Note

Ethics is the one field of study that we all need. This is because we all make choices and ethics is about the general norms that govern how we should make those choices. Not surprisingly, there is disagreement over what those norms are. What this book does is help you to work through that disagreement so that you can then make better choices.

Acknowledgments

I want to thank Oxford University Press and Pearson Education, Inc. for permission to reprint from previous work.

1

Introduction

At first glance, ethics appears to be unlike other areas of inquiry. After all, we cannot find contemporary defenders of Ptolemy (100–70 CE), Copernicus (1473–1543), or Isaac Newton (1642–1727), all claiming to have the best theory of the physics of celestial motion. Nor are there contemporary mercantilists or physiocrats, as there were in the 18th century, all claiming to have the best theory of macroeconomics. However, we can find contemporary defenders of Aristotle (384–322 BCE), Immanuel Kant (1724–1804), and John Stuart Mill (1806–73), for example, all claiming to have the best theory of ethics. While significant disagreements remain in other areas of inquiry, the extent of disagreement appears to be much greater in ethics.

Of course, one explanation for this seemingly greater disagreement is that there is little or nothing that can really be established in ethics. This would explain why so many of the ethical theories that have been proposed in the past continue to have their contemporary defenders. On this account, ethics simply lacks the resources to defeat any of the contending theories, and so they all remain live options. Obviously, this explanation does not put ethics in a very favorable light.

Fortunately, a better explanation is that traditional theories of ethics, whether they justify actions simply in terms of their consequences or not, have come to be revised and reformed in such a way as to make them quite different from the original theories of the philosophers after whom they are still named. While Aristotle endorsed slavery and the subordination of women, and Kant advocated racism as well as the subordination of women, and Mill supported colonialism, it would be difficult to find any contemporary defenders of these philosophers who still endorse these particular views. Contemporary defenders all claim to be defending revised and reformed versions of Aristotle's, Kant's, and Mill's original ethical theories. So this would allow for progress to be made in ethics similar to the progress that has been made in other areas of knowledge. In this regard, then, ethics would be like physics and economics.

The challenge of ethical relativism

Still, it could be argued that ethics is unlike physics and economics in that its requirements are simply the product of a particular culture and therefore are relative to and applicable to just the members of that culture. This is the thesis of ethical or moral relativism.

In support of this view, Herodotus the ancient Greek historian tells a story about Darius the Great, King of Persia (550–486 BCE). In the story, Darius

> summoned the Greeks who happened to be present at his court, and asked them what they would take to eat the dead bodies of their fathers. They replied that they would not do it for any money in the world. Later, in the presence of the Greeks, and through an interpreter, so they could understand what was said, he asked some Indians, of the tribe called Callatiae, who do in fact eat their parents' dead

bodies, what they would take to burn them. They uttered a cry of horror and forbade him to mention such a dreadful thing.[1]

Clearly, the Greeks and the Callatiae of Darius's time approved of their own particular way of showing respect for dead parents and disapproved of the other's way of doing the same as a course of action for themselves.

There are other examples of this sort. Danish explorer Peter Freucher reports on the following practices of the Eskimos or Inuit of the North in the early 20th century:

> When an old man sees the young men go out hunting and cannot himself go along, he is sorry. When he has to ask other people for skins for his clothing, when he cannot ever again be the one to invite the neighbors to eat his game, life is of no value to him. Rheumatism and other ills may plague him and he wants to die. This has been done in different ways in different tribes, but everywhere it is held that if a man feels himself to be a nuisance, his love for his kin, coupled with the sorrow of not being able to take part in the things which are worthwhile, impels him to die. In some tribes, an old man wants his oldest son or favorite daughter to be the one to put the string around his neck and women may sometimes prefer to be stabbed with a dagger into the heart – a thing which is also done by a son or a daughter or whoever [sic] is available for the deed.[2]

Surely, such practices toward the old are quite different from those that prevail in most societies today, and even different from the practices that now prevail among the Inuit. These are the sort of examples that are offered in support of the thesis of ethical relativism.

Yet notice that if we accept the thesis of ethical relativism, we could never justifiably say that the cultural practices of other societies are ethically inferior to our own. The authority of each society's ethical code would extend no further than its own members.

For instance, we could not condemn Nazi Germany for the Holocaust in which 6 million Jews were killed.

Nor could we blame the North American colonists and, later, the citizens of the United States and Canada for the American Holocaust, which by 1890, together with the impact of European diseases, had reduced the North American Indian population by about 98 percent, to 381,000.[3] We also could not blame the Turks for the million Armenians they massacred from 1914 to 1918 or the Khmer Rouge for the million Cambodians who were massacred from 1975 to 1979 under Pol Pot's regime.[4] Obviously, our inability to justifiably condemn any of these acts in the past or present is an undesirable consequence of accepting the thesis of ethical relativism.

In accepting the thesis of ethical relativism, there is also the problem of determining exactly what the requirements of morality are supposed to be relative to. It is said that they are relative to and a product of a particular cultural group. Yet must that group be a society as a whole, or could it be a subgroup of a society? And why can't morality be relative to just each individual? Why can't moral requirements be determined just by each individual's own personal reflection and thereby be relative to and applicable to that individual alone? If we allow all of these possibilities, then, any act (e.g., contract killing) could be wrong from the point of view of some particular society (e.g., U.S. society), right from the point of view of some subgroup of that society (e.g., the Mafia), and wrong again from the point of view of some particular member of that society or other subgroup (e.g., law enforcement officers). But if this were the case, then obviously it would be extremely difficult for us to know what we should do, all things considered.

But is it true?

Yet despite all the difficulties that come with accepting the thesis of ethical relativism, the thesis might still be true.[5] So is there any way to reasonably determine whether the thesis is true?

Consider the practice in the United Kingdom of driving on the left side of the road along with the opposite practice in China of driving on the right side of the road. What does justify these alternative practices? Well, in both countries, traffic must be regulated in some uniform manner to avoid accidents, and each country adopted different practices to achieve that end. Accordingly, citizens of each country can recognize the justification of the other country's rule of the road, even though it differs from their own country's rule. Accordingly, citizens of each country are normally willing to follow the other country's rule when they happen to be driving in that other country – "when in Rome do as the Romans do."

But are the different rules of the road in the United Kingdom and China an example of ethical relativism? It is difficult to see how this could be the case. Surely, ethical relativists must be maintaining that the requirements of morality are a product of the cultural practices of particular societies in some stronger sense than is displayed by our different rules-of-the-road example. There is too much moral agreement here about the justification of each country's rule of the road and about what should be done in practice for this case to count as an example of ethical relativism.

So let's consider the example of the ancient Greeks and the Callatiae we considered earlier. Here both groups wanted to treat their dead respectfully, but they differed about how that should be done. But why did they differ? Most likely they had different religious beliefs about how to show that respect. Religious belief is assumed to be grounded in special revelations and so is not rationally accessible to everyone. Accordingly, if the Greeks had realized this, they would have also realized that they should not have expected the Callatiae to accept their preferred religiously based way of caring for the dead. And the same would hold for the Callatiae. They, too, should not have expected the Greeks to accept their preferred religiously based way of caring for the dead. Since there is no necessity that they all care for their dead in exactly the same way, what both groups should have wanted is for each to be free to respectfully care for their dead in whatever way they prefer. This is because the moral requirement to respectfully care for the dead leaves open the means by which that requirement is to be satisfied, thus making it possible for different religious beliefs to enter into the determination of how to meet it. So here, too, the relativity exhibited in this example is not the right sort needed to show that the thesis of ethical relativism is true. The example is too similar to the different rules-of-the-road example for it to support ethical relativism.

What about the example drawn from the practices of the Inuit of the early 20th century? At first glance, it does seem like we today hold different moral views about how the elderly should behave. Nevertheless, in various cultural traditions, we find many examples of individuals who have become a burden to the group showing a willingness to sacrifice themselves to increase the chances that others will survive. In the early 20th century, in a similar environment, such behavior was displayed by members of the British expedition attempting to reach the South Pole led by Sir Ernest Shackleton,[6] and even more generally, such behavior can be found throughout the history of warfare. We also find that among the Inuit of today, with better means of survival, the elderly no longer utilize their earlier practice. So instead of viewing this case as one where different moral beliefs are simply the product of different cultures, it is better interpreted as a case where the same moral requirement is instantiated differently because of the presence of different opportunities and different material conditions.

In sum, in none of these cases are the moral requirements at issue simply the product of the particular culture. Rather, they are cases in which the same moral requirements are met differently, for appropriate reasons:

- In the first case, British and Chinese drivers are in complete agreement about the justification and application of a rule of the road.
- In the second case, the moral requirement to respect one's dead is met differently by the Greeks and the Callatiae because they have chosen to act on different religious beliefs where there was a moral option to do so.
- In the third case, the same moral requirements pertaining to self-sacrifice, especially when one is a burden to others, are met differently because of different opportunities and different material conditions by the Inuit and others or by the Inuit themselves at one time and then another.

Yet not all purported examples of ethical relativism are like the ones we have just considered. Consider the following three examples:

Rape and marriage. In 1965, Franca Viola from Alcomo, Sicily, broke with a thousand years of Sicilian tradition by refusing to marry a rich man's son after the son had raped her. This son, Filippo Melodia, having failed as a suitor, kidnapped Viola with the help of accomplices and then raped her with the expectation that she would then marry him to avoid the loss of honor to herself and her family that would otherwise result if she were to refuse to do so. But Viola did refuse to marry him, and with the support of her family, she brought charges against Melodia and the other men who assisted him in the kidnapping. Viola and her family were intimidated and ostracized by most of the townspeople. Members of her family received death threats and their barn and vineyard were burned to the ground. But Viola prevailed against Melodia in the trial, and Melodia was sentenced to ten years in prison. Viola later married her childhood sweetheart, who on the day of their wedding felt the need to carry a gun for protection.[7]

Widows and suttee. In 1987 in Deorala, India, an exceptionally beautiful and relatively well-educated eighteen-year-old named Roop Kanwar mounted her husband's funeral pyre and was burned to death. After only eight months of marriage, her husband had died suddenly from appendicitis. She then faced the prospect of spending the rest of her life as a childless widow who could never remarry. She was expected to shave her head, sleep on the floor, wear nothing but the drabbest of clothes, and perform menial tasks. The morning following her husband's death, Kanwar, dressed in her finest wedding sari, led about five hundred of the villagers to the cremation site. With Brahman priests offering prayers, she climbed onto the funeral pyre next to her husband's body, laying his head on her lap. She then signaled to her brother-in-law to light the kindling. Within an hour, Kanwar and her husband were reduced to ashes in accord with the ancient custom of suttee. In the fortnight following her death, 750,000 people turned up to worship at the site of her pyre. Some members of her family and some villagers were later charged with murder, but after nine years of legal proceedings, all were cleared of the charge. Nevertheless, some claimed that her in-laws had pressured her into the suttee and had drugged her with opium. And one unnamed farmer, quoted in a Mumbai newspaper, said that she tried to get off the pyre three times and was pushed back onto it by irate villagers.[8]

A similar practice that developed in China is that of widow chastity. The practice of widow chastity was not new in China even in Song times (960–1279). One source has it that: "According to ritual, husbands have a duty to marry again, but there is no text that authorizes

a woman to remarry."[9] And one neo-Confucian philosopher told his followers that it would be better for
a widow to die of starvation than to lose her virtue
by remarrying.[10] So although most Confucian scholars
and government officials disapproved of the practice,
they often expressed great admiration for women who
abided by the practice, thus helping to perpetuate it. The
practice of widow chastity seems to have come to an end
in China with the collapse of the last imperial dynasty.

Female circumcision: a personal account.

> I will never forget the day of my circumcision which took
> place forty years ago. I was six years old. One morning
> during my school summer vacation, my mother told me
> that I had to go with her to her sisters' house and then to
> visit a sick relative. . . . We did go to my aunts' house and
> from there all of us went straight to [a] red brick house [I
> had never seen].
>
> While my mother was knocking, I tried to pronounce
> the name on the door. Soon enough I realized that it was
> Hajja Alamin's house. She was the midwife who performed
> circumcisions on girls in my neighborhood. I was petrified
> and tried to break loose. But I was captured and subdued
> by my mother and two aunts. They began to tell me that
> the midwife was going to purify me. . . .
>
> The women ordered me to lie down on a bed [made
> of ropes] that had a hole in the middle. They held me
> tight while the midwife started to cut my flesh without
> anesthetics. I screamed till I lost my voice. . . . After the
> job was done, I could not eat, drink or even pass urine
> for three days. I remember that one of my uncles who had
> discovered what they did to me threatened to press charges
> against his sisters. They were afraid of him and they decided
> to bring me back to the midwife. In her sternest voice she
> ordered me to squat on the floor and urinate. It seemed like
> the most difficult thing to do at that point, but I did it. I
> urinated for a long time and shivered with pain.
>
> I understood the motives of my mother, that she wanted
> me to be clean, but I suffered a lot.[11]

In China, the closest practice to female circumcision seems to be that of footbinding, which became popular especially among the wealthy classes during the Song dynasty and only died out in the early 20th century.[12]

In these three cases, unlike our previous examples, the disagreement about what should be done does seem to be more fundamental, and there does not seem to be any agreement about basic moral requirements that lie behind these disagreements. Do these examples, then, support the thesis of ethical relativism? Do these examples suggest that the requirements of morality are simply the product of a particular culture and therefore are relative to and applicable to just the members of that culture? Let's examine each in turn to determine whether this is the case.

Analysis of the case of rape and marriage

In the first case, Franca Viola and her rejected suitor, Filippo Melodia, are in fundamental disagreement about what each of them should or is permitted to do. Yet in order for that disagreement to support the thesis of ethical relativism, it must be grounded in a disagreement over moral requirements or entitlements. This means that in the Sicilian society of his time, Melodia must have been understood to be morally entitled to rape the woman he sought to marry in order to get her to consent to marry him, and Viola, after she was raped, must have been understood to be morally required to marry him. This contrasts, of course, with what obtains in virtually all societies today and even with what obtained in the particular subgroup to which Viola belonged in her day, where rejected suitors were understood to have no such moral entitlements and victims of rape no such moral requirements.

Nevertheless, while Viola and Melodia disagree, it is

not over moral entitlements and moral requirements. Clearly, individuals or groups can disagree with one another without their disagreement being a moral one. So let us see if we can determine when a disagreement over entitlements and requirements is specifically a moral one, first in the case of individuals and then in the case of groups.

In the case of individuals, thinking something is morally right is clearly different from just thinking that you ought to do that thing. You can think that you ought to do something from a purely selfish standpoint. That surely would be different from thinking that you morally ought to do something. To think that you morally ought to do something, you would need to take the interests of others appropriately into account. However, in doing so, you need not regard those interests to be of equal weight to your own. You could favor your own interests, especially your basic interests, over the interests, even over the basic interests, of others in such an appropriate weighing. Even so, in such a moral weighing, it would be inappropriate to prefer your own nonbasic interests over the basic interests of others by aggressing against their basic needs to satisfy your own nonbasic or luxury needs. Of course, this only roughly characterizes the sort of deliberation that must at least implicitly take place when forming a judgment about what you morally ought to do. Yet without this sort of deliberation being at least implicitly involved, the resulting judgment of what you ought to do cannot justifiably be regarded as a moral one.[13]

Taking this into account, what can we say about Melodia's decision to rape Viola to get her to marry him? Did he reach his decision by appropriately weighing his own interests against the interests of Viola? It is very unlikely that Melodia did anything of the sort. At best, he relied on the authority of his own cultural group to justify his actions. Of course, that could have been sufficient if the relevant culture group – Sicilian society as a whole – had already appropriately determined that the norms on which Melodia relied were moral ones.

That consideration brings us to our second question: When are the entitlements and requirements recognized by a social group appropriately determined to be moral ones? More specifically, how could a social group justifiably come to the conclusion that someone in Melodia's situation would be morally entitled to rape Viola to get her to marry him and that someone in Viola's situation would be morally required to marry Melodia after he has raped her? Surely the group would have to deliberate in an appropriate way to justifiably determine what individuals like Melodia and Viola would be morally entitled or required to do in these circumstances. This would require the group to replicate as near as possible the same sort of deliberation that we imagined an individual would be going through when she justifiably reached a judgment about what she morally ought to do. It would thus involve giving appropriate weight to the interests of the different individuals in the social group.

Of course, it would help to do this if those with conflicting interests were in communication so that they could explain the importance of their interests to one another. There would be a need for a fair weighing of the conflicting interests involved, taking into account the relative importance of the interests of different individuals and groups.

Now the laws of a particular society are frequently put forward as an approximation of just such a moral weighing of the relevant conflicting interests of the members of that society, at least insofar as the resolution of those conflicts requires coercive enforcement. Even so, the laws or customs of particular societies can and do fall short of an adequate moral weighing of the relevant conflicting interests in those societies. And sometimes the laws or customs of a society only pay lip service toward achieving that goal. Sometimes, they actually oppose it. When this happens, the related laws or customs of a particular society are clearly not morally justified. Hence, they do not reflect the moral entitlements and requirements that people are obligated to observe.

Nevertheless, people sincerely trying to be moral may still observe such laws, and may even try to get others to observe them as well. This is because doing anything else is likely to turn out to be even more costly to those whose interests have already been unjustly treated by the laws or customs of their society. In so acting, however, they would in no way be conferring moral legitimacy on the oppressive laws or customs under which they are living. They would also be looking for opportunities to open up to reform or drastically change those unjust laws or customs.

Applying these considerations to an evaluation of the laws or customs of Sicilian society on which Melodia relied, it is fairly obvious that the customs of Sicilian society fell far short of adequately taking Viola's interests into account. Viola's interests in not having to marry a man she rejected who had then raped her were not fairly weighed against Melodia's interests in marrying whomever he wanted. Therefore, the customs of Sicilian society at that time did not constitute or reflect the relevant moral entitlements and requirements in this case, and so the conflict between Melodia and Viola is not one between two individuals committed to different moral entitlements and requirements. In fact, the only entitlements and requirements that had any claim to be moral were those supported by Viola in this case. Hence, the conflict between Melodia and Viola is not the right sort of conflict that is needed to support the thesis of ethical relativism.

Analysis of the case of widows and suttee

The case of Roop Kanwar's act of suttee presents a different problem for any attempt to use it to support the thesis of ethical relativism. The problem is that the principal grounds offered to justify her action are simply religious, and these grounds provide no basis for an independent moral justification. According to Hindu religious tradition, when a husband's death preceded that of his wife, she was responsible for his death because of a sin either in this life or in a previous one. As a consequence, only two options were open to her. She could choose suttee and then she, her husband, her husband's family, her mother's family, and her father's family would all be in paradise for 35 million years no matter how sinful any of them had been.[14] Alternatively, she could live the rest of her life out as a penitent sinner, eating no more than one very plain meal a day, performing the most menial tasks, never sleeping in a bed, wearing only the drabbest of clothes, and having her head shaved monthly by an untouchable male barber. Such behavior was said to be required for the sake of her husband's soul and to keep herself from being reborn as a female animal.[15] However, a religious justification, unless supplemented by independent grounds that can support a moral justification, cannot generate the sort of conflict that is needed to defend the thesis of ethical relativism. Ethical relativism requires conflicting moral perspectives.[16]

Nevertheless, there is a moral dimension to the choice Kanwar faced. This is because rather than allowing her the freedom to practice or not practice her religion, the customs of her community forced her to choose between an act of suttee and an austere life as a widow. She lacked the option to not live that austere life prescribed for widows who choose not to commit suttee. The laws of property and employment in her society also left her no such third option. However, coercing people on religious grounds alone thus for reasons that are not generally accessible to everyone involved is morally objectionable. So we do not have here a conflict between two moral perspectives. Rather, we have a religious perspective that lacks a moral justification for its coercive enforcement of very limited options on widows, on the one hand, in conflict with a moral perspective that opposes those very same limited options, on the other. As such this is not the kind of conflict that is needed to support the thesis of ethical relativism.

Analysis of the case of female circumcision

With respect to the case of female circumcision, the following considerations are relevant to determining whether the practice supports the thesis of ethical relativism.

First, there are three main justifications offered for performing various forms of female circumcision:

1 It reduces women's sexual pleasure and thus aids them in resisting illicit acts.[17]
2 It safeguards a woman's virginity, considered essential to her family's ability to arrange her marriage and receive a brideprice, as well as to family honor.[18]
3 It is expected that a woman is to be circumcised to be eligible for marriage.[19]

But do these "justifications" constitute a moral justification for female circumcision? For that to be the case, these justifications would have to be the outcome of a fair evaluation of the interests of men and women, boys and girls. But do these three justifications embody such fairness? Consider this question: If it is good to use female circumcision to reduce women's sexual desire and help them resist illicit acts, why shouldn't something comparable be done to men, like putting some kind of a restraining clamp on men's penises? Actually, it turns out, something comparable is being done to men, although not intentionally, but rather as the unforeseen

consequence of actions that are undertaken for other
purposes.

Here are the facts. About 12 million males are circumcised yearly (compared to 2 million females). In the
United States, 79% of adult men have been circumcised.
While male circumcision usually involves just removing
the foreskin of the penis, we know now that the foreskin
contains the greatest concentrations of nerve endings.[20]
So its removal should, as with the removal of a woman's
clitoris, similarly be expected to reduce male capacity for sexual pleasure. Yet reducing sexual pleasure,
and thereby decreasing men's desire for it, is definitely
not the reason that is usually given for the practice.
Moreover, if this likely effect of male circumcision were
more generally known, we might reasonably expect a
steep decline in the practice. Hence, the basic unfairness
remains: intentionally imposing the burden of circumcision on women in order to reduce their sexual desire
and thereby aid them in resisting illicit acts while not
intentionally imposing any comparable burden on men
to achieve that same effect.

In order, therefore, for this drastic step to ensure
female purity (virginity before marriage, fidelity after
it) to be morally justified, a comparably drastic step
would need to be taken to ensure male purity as well.
Of course, this is not to say that female circumcision
would be morally justified if a comparably drastic step
were taken to ensure male purity. It is just that without
the burden of a comparable practice being intentionally
imposed on men, intentionally imposing the burden of
this practice on women cannot even begin to be morally
justified.

Nevertheless, when the practice is widespread, it can
be difficult for families not to circumcise their daughters. Not doing so reduces their daughters' prospects for
marriage in a context where the prospects for unmar-
ried women are even more undesirable. Accordingly,
if undergoing some form of circumcision is expected

for a woman to be an eligible marriage partner (some countries have female circumcision rates of between 94 and 98%[21]), a woman who is not circumcised can be at an enormous disadvantage. Hence, you can understand the willingness of parents to circumcise their daughters in such societies, because the consequences of not doing so are so much worse.

The actions undertaken here are analogous to those undertaken by other people attempting to cope with different unjust laws or customs in their societies. Sometimes people will have no real option but to obey those unjust laws or customs themselves and to help to get others to do so as well, because the consequences of not doing so for those suffering from the injustice would be far worse. Even so, while going along with such unjust laws or customs, there is a need to constantly be on the lookout for ways to evade, reform, or drastically change those laws or customs whenever possible.

Nevertheless, the willingness of good people to go along with the practice of female circumcision under unjust conditions because the consequences of not doing so are far worse does not provide a moral justification for the practice, and hence the conflict that individuals and groups experience with respect to the practice cannot, therefore, be used to support the thesis of ethical relativism.

Our six purported cases of ethical relativism

So, let's review the analyses of the six cases we have been considering:

1 *The different rules of the road in the United Kingdom and China.* Analysis: There is too much moral agreement here about the justification for the rules of the road and about what should be done in practice for this case to count as an example of moral conflict.

2 *The different ways of caring for their dead of the ancient Greeks and the Callatiae.* Analysis: Both groups wanted to treat their dead respectfully. Their actions were grounded in the same moral belief. They should have also recognized that given that morality does not establish one way to treat one's dead respectfully, people can legitimately use their different religious traditions to specify what they should do in this regard. There is no moral conflict here.

3 *The different ways Inuit elderly of the early 20th century behaved and our elderly and the Inuit elderly of today behave.* Analysis: The same moral requirements pertaining to self-sacrifice, especially when one is a burden to others, seem to be met differently because of different opportunities and different material conditions that obtain in these different historical periods. There is, then, no moral conflict between what the Inuit elderly did in the past and what is done today.

4 *The different views of Filippo Melodia and Franca Viola concerning the legitimacy and proper response to the rape and a subsequent marriage proposal from a rejected suitor.* Analysis: Melodia and the Sicilian society on which he relied failed to do a fair evaluation of the competing interests involved in this case. Only Viola and those who supported her acted upon a fair evaluation of the competing interests. There was no moral conflict about what should be done.

5 *The different views over whether Roop Kanwar should have been coerced to burn herself to death in an act of suttee.* Analysis: The only justification for coercing Kanwar to perform an act of suttee provided here is religious, so coercing her was not supported by the generally accessible reasons required by morality. Hence there is no moral conflict here that is required for a case of ethical relativism. Here all we have are moral reasons

that condemn the way Kanwar's options to engaging in suttee were so severely limited.

6 *Different views over whether female circumcision should be practiced.* Analysis: The justifications offered for the practice of female circumcision do not meet the requirements for a moral justification. In an unjust society, where the practice is widespread, however, there is a moral justification for going along with the practice to avoid even worse consequences. This does not, however, constitute a moral justification for the practice. The practice does not have a moral justification. Nor is it clear how the practice could be made to be morally justified by creating a parallel practice for men.

Conclusion

Summarizing our six examples, we have failed to uncover any case that supports the thesis of ethical relativism: the view that the requirements of morality are simply the product of a particular culture and therefore are relative to and applicable to only the members of that culture. To support this thesis, what we needed to find were cases of moral conflict that is grounded simply in cultural conflict. What we found in three of our six cases is far too much agreement about what is appropriate behavior to constitute cases of moral conflict. In the other three cases, we did find significant disagreement, but it was not the kind of disagreement that could be characterized as moral conflict. This left the thesis of ethical relativism unsupported.

Nevertheless, it might still be objected that in today's society the case of abortion supports ethical relativism. Clearly, both those who endorse a pro-life position on abortion and those who endorse a pro-choice position on abortion claim to be fairly taking all the relevant interests into account. Yet each side ends up favoring opposing views on the legal permissibility of abortion. So why doesn't this qualify as a case of ethical relativism?

One reason for thinking that is not a case of ethical relativism is that neither side in the debate over abortion would accept the resolution of the debate that would be provided to them by ethical relativism. Neither side would think that the culture they happen to be living in is the proper determinant of whether abortions should be prohibited or not. Rather, both sides claim that there are reasons accessible to all for favoring their preferred resolution of the debate. Those on the pro-life side think that morality provides both sides with accessible reasons for favoring their pro-life position and those on the pro-choice side think just the opposite.

Nevertheless, both views cannot be right. If we reject ethical relativism, either abortion is justifiably legally permitted or it is justifiably legally prohibited. It cannot be both. Abortion, or at least the same kind of abortion, cannot be both justifiably legally permitted and justifiably legally prohibited in the same place and at the same time. Hence, in the case of abortion, one side or the other must have successfully taken into account all the relevant interests in order to determine whether abortion is to be justifiably legally prohibited or not.[22] So while it is difficult to determine which side that is, this difficulty does not support the thesis of ethical relativism, at least as judged by those who hold the opposing views in this debate.

Yet to completely defeat ethical relativism, we must do more than defeat examples that purport to support the view. To completely defeat ethical relativism, we need a positive defense of morality, where morality is understood, as it was in this chapter, as the practice of appropriately or fairly taking into account the interests of all those affected. Happily, just such a defense is proposed at the end of the next chapter.

2

Why be Moral?

Turning now to the justification for being moral, we find in Plato's *The Republic* (c. 380 BCE) a story about Gyges, a shepherd in the service of the King of Lydia (in modern-day Turkey), who happened upon a ring that when worn and turned in one direction made him invisible and when turned back made him visible again. Once Gyges became aware of the power of the ring, he arranged to be sent as a messenger to the king. On arriving at the palace, he committed adultery with the queen, killed the king with her help, and took over the kingdom.[1]

From Plato's time to the present, this story has helped to dramatically ask the question: Why should I be just or moral when I could really benefit myself more from doing something else? In everyday life, this question suggests the following:

- Why should I help people in serious need when I can use my extra income to dine in a fancy restaurant or take a Scandinavian cruise?
- Why should I not cheat on my taxes if I can get away with it?

- Why should I limit my use of earth's resources now so that future generations can have a decent life?

These questions express the fundamental challenge that egoism raises to morality.

Ethical egoism

In Plato's Gyges story, the question is posed: Why should Gyges be moral or just when, given his magical ring, he could benefit more by acting self-interestedly? Yet we do not have to reach back to Plato, or to myth, to find examples of egoism raising a challenge to morality.

On December 10, 2008, Bernard Madoff, the former chair of the NASDAQ Stock Market, revealed to his two sons that the investment management arm of his firm was a giant Ponzi scheme – as he put it, "one big lie." A Ponzi scheme is a fraudulent investment operation that pays returns to investors from their own money or from money contributed by subsequent investors rather than from profit, and as a result, at some point the scheme has to run out of money.[2] After Madoff's sons passed on this information to the authorities, Madoff was arrested and charged with bilking his investors out of $50 billion. That made his crime the largest Ponzi scheme ever perpetrated and the largest investment fraud ever committed by a single person. By targeting charities, Madoff was also able to avoid the threat of sudden or unexpected withdrawals and so he was able to keep his scheme going for a number of years.[3]

Surely Madoff's behavior should suffice to make him an egoist. Even so, as an egoist, he did make one fairly significant mistake. He didn't find a way to disappear with a significant portion of his stolen funds just before his Ponzi scheme collapsed. However, the question we need to focus on is: How does egoism purport to justify the behavior of Gyges and Madoff and many other egoists like them?

To answer this question, we need to consider the two main forms that egoism takes:

1 Individual Ethical Egoism: this holds that everyone *ought* to do what is in the overall self-interest of just one particular individual.[4]
2 Universal Ethical Egoism: this holds that everyone *ought* to do what is in his or her own overall self-interest.

Individual Ethical Egoism

Let's begin by addressing the challenge of Individual Ethical Egoism, a view that is often not clearly distinguished from the more discussed Universal Ethical Egoism.[5] Individual Ethical Egoism maintains that everyone ought to do what is in the overall self-interest of just one particular individual. That means that all claims about what each of us ought to do are to be based on the overall interests of just one particular individual. The good of that one individual determines what everyone else ought to do.

Let's call that individual Penelope. Why do only Penelope's interests count in determining what everyone ought to do? Individual Ethical Egoism must provide us with an adequate justification for giving only Penelope's interests this status.

Consider what will *not* work to provide such a justification:

1 Any *relational characteristic*, such as Penelope being Yufeng's wife, would not provide justification for Penelope's special status, because other persons would have similar relational characteristics.

2 Any *characteristic shared with others*, like being a woman or a feminist, would not justify favoring Penelope's interests, because it would not provide the same justification for favoring the interests of all other women or feminists.

3 Any *unique characteristic*, such as Penelope knowing all of Shakespeare's writings by heart, would not provide justification, because others may possess such characteristics to lesser degrees, giving them justification (although proportionally less) for favoring their own interests.

4 The mere fact of *possessing unique traits* would not justify Penelope's special status, because every individual has unique traits.

5 *Claiming special status* simply because Penelope is herself and wants to further her own interests would not provide justification, because every other person could make the same claim.

In sum, if the defender of Individual Ethical Egoism were to argue that the same or similar reasons do *not* hold for other people with the same or similar characteristics to those of Penelope, the defender must explain *why* they do not hold. This is because it must always be possible to understand how a characteristic serves as a reason in one case but not in another. If no explanation can be provided, and in the case of Individual Ethical Egoism none has been forthcoming, the proposed characteristic either serves as a reason in both cases or it does not serve as a reason at all.

Thus, it turns out that Individual Ethical Egoism, upon examination, is an indefensible position. It claims that everyone ought to do what serves the overall interest of just one particular individual, but it is incapable of providing any justification which could plausibly support that claim.

Universal Ethical Egoism

The Universal Ethical Egoist (let's call him Yufeng) presumably starts out with the same general goal as Penelope, whose interests were to be served by Individual Ethical Egoism. Yufeng, too, would like to show that the furthering of his own interests is the thing to do. Nevertheless, he recognizes that any reason that he could give for furthering his own interests would suggest a similar or analogous reason that others could give for furthering their interests. As a Universal Ethical Egoist, however, Yufeng confronts this problem by granting that each person has similar reasons for favoring his or her own interests. In order to justify favoring his own interests, Yufeng realizes that he must allow that others are similarly justified in favoring their own interests. It is this willingness to generalize that saves Universal Ethical Egoism from the fate of Individual Ethical Egoism, which refused to generalize, thereby rendering Universal Ethical Egoism a serious challenge to morality. Let us now consider three of the most important attempts to meet that challenge.

Appealing to publicity

Universal Ethical Egoism has been forcefully criticized by contemporary philosopher Christine Korsgaard, among others, for failing to meet a "publicity requirement" that is satisfied by morality.[6] Those committed to morality, just like those committed to obeying the law, usually want their commitment to be publicly known so that they will be better able to resolve conflicts with others who are similarly committed. By contrast, Yufeng, our Universal Ethical Egoist, is usually not going to want his commitment to Universal Ethical Egoism to be publicly known. If others know that he is an egoist, they will

tend to guard themselves against being harmed by him
and, as a consequence, he may not be able to benefit
at their expense to the degree that he would otherwise
want to do. Rather, while privately endorsing egoism,
Yufeng is going to publicly, yet hypocritically, profess a
commitment to morality in order to secure for himself
the benefit that such a public endorsement of morality
provides.

Of course, privately, Yufeng thinks that others, like
him, ought to be similarly committed to Universal
Ethical Egoism, although he will never tell them so,
except perhaps when their interests happen to further
his own. For him to reveal his commitment to Universal
Ethical Egoism on other occasions would work against
his interests. There will be times when Yufeng will think
that others ought to interfere with him, yet because he
and others are publicly committed to a morality that prohibits and attempts to punish interferences of this sort, he
will thereby hope to avoid such interference to himself.
On other occasions, Yufeng will be able to further his
overall self-interest by selectively, and usually secretively,
interfering with the interests of others in violation of the
requirements of morality. This is exactly what Gyges was
able to do in Plato's dialogue, and what Madoff was able
to do in real life as well, at least for a number of years.
So while Universal Ethical Egoism is not committed to
the same publicity requirement that we find in morality,
given its rationale for avoiding that requirement, it is difficult to see how this lack of commitment should count
as grounds for rejecting the view. Clearly, keeping their
commitment to egoism relatively private was essential to
the success of both Gyges and Madoff.[7]

Paralleling egoism and racism

Now James Rachels offers an argument that he thinks
comes closest to an outright refutation of Ethical

Egoism.[8] Rachels attempts to defeat egoism by paralleling the view with racism and then showing that they are similarly defective. He argues that just as the racist does not provide a good reason why everyone should support the racist's own preferred racial group, so the egoist does not provide a good reason why everyone should support the egoist's own interests over everyone else's interests.

Unfortunately, while Rachels directs his argument against egoism generally, his argument works only against Individual Ethical Egoism. It does not also work against Universal Ethical Egoism, the view that we are presently considering.[9] This is because only Individual Ethical Egoism wants to defend putting someone, and by extension some group, in a special category. Universal Ethical Egoism, by contrast, wants to treat everyone the same, at least to the extent of allowing that everyone is equally justified in pursuing his or her own self-interest. So, while Rachels's argument does work against Individual Ethical Egoism, it fails to meet the more serious challenge of Universal Ethical Egoism.

Appealing to consistency

Still another attempt to meet the challenge of Universal Ethical Egoism, advanced by Kurt Baier, tries to show that the view is fundamentally inconsistent.[10] For the purpose of evaluating this critique, let's use as an example a modern Gyges, Gary Gyges by name, an otherwise normal human being who, for reasons of personal gain, has embezzled $10 million while working as an accountant at People's National Bank and is now taking steps to escape to a South Sea island where he will have the good fortune to live a pleasant life protected by the local authorities and untroubled by any qualms of conscience. Suppose that a fellow employee, Hedda Hawkeye, knows that Gyges has embezzled money from the bank and that he is about to escape. Suppose, further, that it is in Hawkeye's overall self-interest to prevent Gyges from escaping with the embezzled money because she will be generously rewarded for doing so by being appointed vice president of the bank. Given that it is in Gyges's overall self-interest to escape with the embezzled money, it now appears that we can derive a contradiction for Universal Ethical Egoism from the following:

1 Gyges ought to escape with the embezzled money.
2 Hawkeye ought to prevent Gyges from escaping with the embezzled money.
3 By preventing Gyges from escaping with the embezzled money, Hawkeye is preventing Gyges from doing what he ought to do.
4 One ought never to prevent someone from doing what he or she ought to do.
5 Thus, Hawkeye ought not to prevent Gyges from escaping with the embezzled money.

Because premise (2) and conclusion (5) are contradictory, Universal Ethical Egoism appears to be inconsistent.

The soundness of this argument depends, however, on premise (4), and Yufeng, our Universal Ethical Egoist, believes there are grounds for rejecting this premise. As Yufeng understands the "oughts" of Universal Ethical Egoism, he is justified in preventing others from doing what they ought to do in violation of premise (4). This is because Yufeng understands them to be analogous to the "oughts" of competitive games, which do justify just this sort of behavior.

Consider, for example, how in football a defensive player might think that the opposing team's quarterback ought to pass on third down with five yards to go, while not wanting the quarterback to do so and indeed hoping to foil any such attempt the quarterback makes. Or to use Jesse Kalin's example:

I may see how my chess opponent can put my king in check. This is how he ought to move. But believing that he ought to move his bishop and check my king does not commit me to wanting him to do that, nor to persuading him to do so. What I ought to do is sit there quietly, hoping he does not move as he ought.[11]

The point of these examples is to suggest that a Universal Ethical Egoist may, like a player in a game, judge that others ought to do what is in their overall self-interest while simultaneously attempting to prevent such actions or at least refraining from encouraging them. And this provides grounds for rejecting premise (4) from the earlier argument against Universal Ethical Egoism.

The analogy of competitive games also illustrates the sense in which a Universal Ethical Egoist claims that she herself ought to do what is in her overall self-interest. For just as a player's judgment that she ought to make a particular move is followed, other things being equal, by an attempt to perform the appropriate action (the defensive player attempting to stop the quarterback's throw), so likewise when a Universal Ethical Egoist judges that she ought to do some particular action, other things being equal, an attempt to perform the appropriate action follows (Madoff's attempt to benefit indefinitely from his Ponzi scheme).

In general, defenders of Universal Ethical Egoism stress that because we have little difficulty understanding the implications of the use of "ought" in competitive games, we should also have little difficulty understanding the analogous use of "ought" by the Universal Ethical Egoist, which in turn provides grounds for rejecting premise (4) of the argument that was supposed to show that Universal Ethical Egoism was an inconsistent view.[12]

Is there no way to meet the challenge of Universal Ethical Egoism?

The challenge of Universal Ethical Egoism to morality has proven to be a strong one, as the failure of the previous three arguments to meet that challenge indicates. In fact, owing to past failures to provide a strong defense of morality over egoism, most moral philosophers today have simply given up hope of providing an argument showing that morality is rationally preferable to egoism.[13] Rather, they seem content to show that morality is simply rationally permissible, which implies that egoism is rationally permissible as well. Most contemporary moral philosophers do not think anything more can be established.

While this consensus among moral philosophers today is quite strong, a few philosophers express hope that we can do better and actually provide arguments showing that morality is rationally required and not just simply rationally permissible.[14] Most moral philosophers today would certainly like to have a good argument of this sort. So given the importance of the question of whether morality can be shown to be rationally required, let us consider just one more attempt to meet the challenge of Universal Ethical Egoism and show that morality is rationally preferable to it.

From rationality to morality

Let us begin by imagining that each of us is capable of entertaining and acting upon both self-interested and moral reasons and that the question we are seeking to answer is what sort of reasons for action it would be rational for us to accept.[15] This question is not about what sort of reasons we should publicly affirm, since people will sometimes publicly affirm reasons that are quite different from those they are prepared to act upon. Rather, this question focuses on what reasons it would be rational for us to accept at the deepest level – in our heart of hearts – when we are speaking truthfully to ourselves.

Granted, some people are incapable of acting upon moral reasons. For such people, there is no question about their being required to act morally or altruistically. Yet the interesting philosophical question is not about them but about people, like ourselves, who are capable of acting morally as well as self-interestedly and are seeking a rational justification for following a particular course of action.

In trying to determine how we should act, let us assume that we would like to be able to construct a good argument favoring morality over egoism. Given that good arguments are nonquestion-begging, they do not assume what they are trying to prove.

In a film by Sacha Guitry, *The Pearls of the Crown* (1937), three thieves are arguing over the division of some valuable pearls. One of these thieves gives two to the thief on his right, then two to the thief on his left. "I," he says, "will keep three." "How come you get to keep three?" one of the other thieves asks. "Because I am the leader," he replies. "Oh. But how come you are the leader?" asks the other thief. "Because I have more pearls," he replies. In the film, this question-begging argument, which assumes just what it purports to prove, surprisingly satisfies the other two thieves because they do not further question how the pearls have been distributed. Nevertheless, let's assume that we would like to do better by constructing a good argument for morality that does not similarly beg the question.

The question at issue here is what reasons each of us should take as supreme, and this question would be begged against Universal Ethical Egoism (hereafter simply egoism) if we proposed to answer it simply by assuming from the start that moral reasons are the reasons that each of us should take as supreme. But the question would be begged against morality as well if we proposed to answer the question simply by assuming from the start that self-interested reasons are the reasons that each of us should take as supreme. This means, of course, that we cannot answer the question of what reasons we should take as supreme simply by assuming the general principle of egoism: *Each person ought to do what best serves his or her overall self-interest.* We can no more argue for egoism simply by denying the relevance of moral reasons to rational choice than we can argue for altruism simply by denying the relevance of self-interested reasons to rational choice and assuming the general principle of altruism: *Each person ought to do what best serves the overall interest of others.*[16] Consequently, we have no other alternative but to grant the prima facie relevance of both self-interested and altruistic reasons to rational choice and then try to determine which reasons we would be rationally required to act upon, all things considered. (Notice that in order not to beg the question, it is necessary to back off from both the general principle of egoism and the general principle of altruism. From this standpoint, it is still an open question whether egoism or altruism will be rationally preferable.)

This leaves us to consider two kinds of cases: cases in which there is a conflict between the relevant self-interested and moral or altruistic reasons, and cases in which there is no such conflict.

It seems obvious that where there is no conflict and both reasons are conclusive reasons of their kind, both reasons should be acted upon. In such contexts, we should do what is favored both by morality or altruism and by self-interest.

Consider the following example. Suppose you accepted a job marketing a baby formula in a developing country where the formula was improperly used, leading to increased infant mortality.[17] Imagine that you could just as well have accepted an equally attractive and rewarding job marketing a similar formula in a developed country where the misuse does not occur, so that a rational weighing of the relevant self-interested reasons alone would not have favored your acceptance of one of these jobs over the other.[18] At the same time, there were obviously moral reasons that condemned your acceptance of the first job – reasons that you presumably are or were able to acquire. Moreover, by assumption in this case, the moral reasons do not clash with the relevant self-interested reasons: they simply made a recommendation where the relevant self-interested reasons were silent. Consequently, a rational weighing of all the relevant reasons in this case could not but favor acting in accord with both the relevant self-interested and moral reasons.

Now when we rationally assess the relevant reasons in conflict cases, it is best to cast the conflict not as one between self-interested reasons and moral reasons but instead as one between self-interested reasons and altruistic reasons.[19] Viewed in this way, three solutions are possible:

1 Self-interested reasons always have priority over conflicting altruistic reasons.
2 Altruistic reasons always have priority over conflicting self-interested reasons.
3 Some kind of compromise is rationally required. In this compromise, sometimes self-interested reasons would have priority over altruistic reasons, and sometimes altruistic reasons would have priority over self-interested reasons.

Once the conflict is described in this manner, the third solution can be seen to be the one that is rationally required. This is because the first and second solutions give exclusive priority to one class of relevant reasons over the other, and only a question-begging justification can be given for such an exclusive priority. Only by

employing the third solution – sometimes giving priority
to self-interested reasons, sometimes giving priority to
altruistic reasons – can we avoid a question-begging
resolution.

For example, suppose that you are in the waste disposal business and you have decided to dispose of toxic
wastes in a manner that is cost-efficient for you but pre-
dictably causes significant harm to future generations.
Imagine that there are alternative methods available
for disposing of the wastes that are only slightly less
cost-efficient and will not cause any significant harm to
future generations.[20] In this case, you would weigh your
self-interested reasons favoring the most cost-efficient
disposal of the toxic wastes against the relevant altruistic reasons favoring the avoidance of significant harm
to future generations. If we suppose that the projected
loss of benefit to yourself was ever so slight and the projected harm to future generations was ever so great, then
a nonarbitrary compromise between the relevant self-
interested and altruistic reasons would have to favor the
altruistic reasons. Hence, as judged by a nonquestion-
begging standard of rationality, your method of waste
disposal was contrary to the relevant reasons.

Notice also that this standard of rationality will not
support just any compromise between the relevant self-
interested and altruistic reasons. The compromise must
be a nonarbitrary one, for otherwise it would beg the
question with respect to the opposing egoistic or altruistic perspective.[21] Such a compromise would have to
respect the rankings of self-interested and altruistic reasons imposed by the egoistic and altruistic perspectives,
respectively. Accordingly, any nonarbitrary compromise
among such reasons in seeking not to beg the question
against either egoism or altruism will have to give priority to those reasons that rank highest in each category.
Failure to give priority to the highest-ranking altruistic
or self-interested reasons would, other things being
equal, be contrary to reason.

Lifeboat cases

Of course, there will be cases in which the only way to avoid being required to do what is contrary to your highest-ranking reasons is by requiring someone else to do what is contrary to his or her highest-ranking reasons. Some of these cases will be so-called lifeboat cases, as when two individuals are stranded in a lifeboat that has only enough resources for one to survive. Although such cases are surely difficult to resolve (maybe only a chance mechanism, like flipping a coin, can offer a reasonable resolution), they surely do not reflect the typical conflict between the relevant self-interested and altruistic reasons that we are or were able to acquire.

Morality as Compromise

We can see how morality can be viewed as a nonarbitrary compromise between self-interested and altruistic reasons. First, a certain amount of self-regard is morally required or at least morally acceptable. Where this is the case, high-ranking self-interested reasons have priority over low-ranking altruistic reasons. Second, morality obviously places limits on the extent to which people should pursue their own self-interest. Where this is the case, high-ranking altruistic reasons have priority over low-ranking self-interested reasons. In this way, morality can be seen to be a nonarbitrary compromise between self-interested and altruistic reasons, and the "moral reasons" that constitute that compromise can be seen as having an absolute priority over the self-interested or altruistic reasons that conflict with them.[22]

Yet does Morality as Compromise provide an answer to the egoism as practiced by Gyges in myth and by

Madoff in reality? Well, it does provide a good – that is, a nonquestion-begging – argument favoring morality over egoism and in this way justifies morality over egoism. Of course, this may not have the hoped-for effect on real-life egoists. They may not care whether there is a good argument or justification for what they are doing or proposing to do. To deal with them, we may have to resort to avoidance or coercion. If we do need to resort to coercion, however, Morality as Compromise can also provide us with a good argument for doing so. What more could we expect it to do to meet the challenge of egoism?

Of course, exactly how Morality as Compromise is to be implemented in practice needs to be determined. So far developed, it is open to a number of different interpretations. A consequentialist approach would presumably favor one sort of interpretation of the compromise, a nonconsequentialist approach of either a Kantian or Aristotelian variety would presumably favor yet another, as we will see in subsequent chapters. So Morality as Compromise is anything but a decision procedure for solving practical moral problems. Nevertheless, however this debate between alternative interpretations is resolved, it is clear that some sort of a compromise view or moral solution is rationally preferable to either egoism or altruism when judged from a nonquestion-begging standpoint. Surely, that should suffice to answer the challenge of egoism.

Conclusion

In this chapter, we have seen that the challenge of Individual Ethical Egoism showed itself to be incapable of providing any justification that could plausibly support the view. By contrast, Universal Ethical Egoism showed itself a formidable challenge to ethics, easily turning aside objections appealing to the publicity of reasons, to parallels between egoism and racism, and to consistency. This challenge, as we saw, could only effectively be met by a nonquestion-begging argument that favored morality over both egoism and altruism.

3

Consequentialism

The first Sunday after 9/11, then U.S. Vice President Dick Cheney, appearing on *Meet the Press*, gave a memorable statement of how the Bush administration planned to deal with the threat posed by the terrorist attacks on the World Trade Center and the Pentagon:

> We'll have to work sort of the dark side, if you will. We've got to spend time in the shadows in the intelligence world. A lot of what needs to be done here will have to be done quietly, without any discussion, using sources and methods that are available to our intelligence agencies – if we are to be successful. That's the world these folks operate in. . . . [S]o it's going to be vital for us to use any means at our disposal basically, to achieve our objectives.[1]

We now know a lot more of what Cheney meant by this shift in U.S. policy following 9/11 and what British support for that policy meant as well.[2] It involved releasing military forces, the CIA in particular, from the constraints of the Geneva Conventions. Under the Geneva Conventions, detainees had to be treated humanely.[3] Prisoners of war could not be punished for refusing to cooperate with interrogators and they had to be given

access to the Red Cross. "No physical or mental torture or any other form of coercion may be inflicted
on prisoners of war to secure from them information
of any kind whatsoever," the Geneva Conventions
stated. Moreover, every captive was entitled to a hear-
ing before a competent tribunal in order to determine
his or her status. Even during the Vietnam War, when
the North Vietnamese refused to regard U.S. pilots, like
John McCain, as legitimately covered by the Geneva
Conventions, calling them "pirates" in an illegal war,
thus, in the minds of the Vietcong, permitting their use
of torture to obtain information, the United States con-
tinued to respect the Geneva Conventions as applying to
its opponents.

In addition, although the UN Convention Against
Torture prohibited any signee from "expelling, extradit-
ing or otherwise effecting the involuntary removal of any
person to a country where there are substantial grounds
for believing the person would be in danger of being
subject to torture," the Bush administration, following
9/11, with the support of the Blair administration, regu-
larly availed itself of such renditions to states like Egypt,
Monaco, Syria, Jordan, Uzbekistan, and Afghanistan,
all of which were known, at the time, to torture and had
long been cited by the U.S. State Department for human
rights violations. Syria, for example, was known for
"administering electric shocks, pulling out finger nails,
forcing objects up the rectum and hyper-extending the
spine" to the point of "fracture." In Egypt, detainees
"were stripped and blindfolded, suspended from a
ceiling or door frame with feet just touching the floor;
beaten with fists, whips, metal rods, or other objects;
subjected to electric shocks, and doused with cold water
[and] sexually assaulted."

Introducing consequentialist ethics

One ethical theory that may, however, justify such acts of torture is consequentialism, which was first proposed by Mo Tzu in China around 450 BCE, and for a time presented a challenge to the dominant Confucianism. In the West, however, the theory traces its origins to Francis Hutchinson (1723–90) and David Hume (1711–76), and its most canonical formulations are found in the work of Jeremy Bentham (1748–1832) and John Stuart Mill (1806–73). In 1806, a meeting between Bentham and James Mill (John Stuart Mill's father) led to the formation of a group called the Philosophical Radicals, who pressed for political and social reforms in the UK. John Stuart Mill, a child prodigy, studied Greek at three, Latin at eight, wrote a history of Roman law at ten, and at fifteen undertook a study of Bentham's writings. Later, guided by his father, he became intensely involved in the work of the Philosophical Radicals.

For Bentham, there was only one ultimate principle of morality, namely, the Principle of Utility, which requires us to always choose whatever action or social policy would have the best consequences for everyone concerned. As he put it in his book *An Introduction to the Principles of Morals and Legislation*: "By the Principle of Utility is meant that principle which approves or disapproves of every action whatsoever, according to the tendency which it appears to have to augment or diminish the happiness of the party whose interest is in question."[4] But who is "the party whose interest is in question" for consequentialists? Mill made it perfectly clear that it was everyone who could be affected by the action in question: "[T]he happiness which forms the utilitarian standard of what is right in conduct . . . is not the agent's own happiness but that of all concerned. As between his own happiness and that of others, utilitarianism requires him to be strictly impartial as a disinterested and benevolent spectator."[5]

In his own day, Bentham appealed to this consequentialist standard to support the separation of church and state, freedom of expression, the end of slavery, free trade, the decriminalization of homosexuality, and the elimination of the death penalty. Mill also used it to support universal male suffrage, proportional representation, labor unions, and farm cooperatives. In 1869, Mill also published *The Subjection of Women*, in which he argued for gender equality on consequentialist grounds.

Bentham understood happiness to be pleasure, and he took pleasures not to differ in quality. Thus, he famously remarked that pushpin (a children's game) is as good as poetry, in that, as Bentham saw it, they both provided the same kind of pleasure.[6] While Mill, too, equated happiness with pleasure, he disagreed with Bentham by holding that pleasures can vary in quality. According to Mill, playing pushpin and reading Shakespearean sonnets provided qualitatively different kinds of pleasure. Mill also held that qualitatively higher pleasures were those that would be preferred by competent judges who had experienced the alternatives. Applying this standard, Mill also famously claimed that "it is better to be a human being dissatisfied than a pig satisfied; better to be Socrates dissatisfied than a fool satisfied."[7] Of course, no competent human judge, as far as we know, has become a real pig and then returned to human form to tell us what that experience was like. Accordingly, what Mill must have been doing here is simply berating fellow humans, who, unlike real pigs, fail to take advantage of the full range of pleasures available to them.

Still, critics have pointed out that other things contribute to our good, and so to our happiness, which are not pleasures that we personally experience. For example, when someone is prevented from slandering us, our good is served, even if we would never hear about the slander or experience its effects. We also think it is important to maintain certain relationships with others, particularly friendships, at least in part, irrespective of any pleasures that we or anyone else happen to derive from them. Accordingly, contemporary consequential-ists have come to understand happiness more broadly than Bentham and Mill to include anything that contrib-utes to our good or to the good of others, and this is why the view is better characterized as consequentialism than as utilitarianism because the latter designation tends to be associated with just an assessment of pleasures and pains.

An implication of consequentialist ethics: sacrificing the few for the many

Yet whether a person's happiness is understood broadly or narrowly, consequentialists have always allowed that the happiness or good of a few can be sacrificed if it results in greater good for the many, and so greater good overall. Drawing on David Hume, contemporary defenders of consequentialist ethics sometimes claim that what consequentialism requires is what an ide-ally sympathetic agent, with knowledge of everyone's interests, would approve of. Accordingly, it would be permissible, according to consequentialism, to tax the rich to secure a decent minimum for the poor, pro-vided that the benefit to the poor is greater than any consequentialist loss to the rich.

So why couldn't consequentialism be similarly used to justify the practice of torturing detainees as a way of achieving a greater good overall? One could ques-tion whether the actions that the Bush administration authorized against detainees with support from the Blair administration did, in fact, constitute torture. What was authorized did include such practices as waterboarding, or producing the sensations of drowning or suffocation, which had long been thought to be torture under the Geneva Conventions and had been prosecuted as such after World War II at the Tokyo Trials and by the United States as recently as 1983.

Yet Bush administration lawyers redefined torture so that waterboarding in itself did not constitute torture. According to Jay Bybee, at the time the head of the Office of Legal Counsel in the U.S. Department of Justice and now a U.S. federal judge, "physical pain amounting to torture must be equivalent in intensity to the pain accompanying serious physical injury, such as organ failure, impairment of bodily function or even death," and "for purely mental pain or suffering to amount to torture, it must result in significant psychological harm of significant duration, e.g., lasting months or even years."[8] So maybe what was done to detainees did not constitute torture so defined.

But let's not go against long-standing internationally recognized definitions of torture here. Let us allow that waterboarding is torture and then ask whether it, or even worse impositions, could be justified by the good outcome that would result from subjecting detainees to such treatment.[9] Presumably the justification was to extract information from detainees that could be used to prevent further harm to the United States, the United Kingdom, and their citizens.[10] Of course, detainees would suffer from being tortured, but the compensating benefit to others would be understood to justify that suffering. That is how a consequentialist justification might be given for the use of torture in Guantánamo, Abu Ghraib, or in any of the black site detention centers to which detainees were sent for interrogation after 9/11.

Osama bin Laden and terrorism

Yet if we could justify the torture of detainees on the basis of the overall good consequences that could reasonably be expected to result, why could not acts of terrorism be similarly justified on the same consequentialist basis?

Consider that act of terrorism of 9/11. That act began on a clear, early autumn morning in New York City. At 8:45 a.m., a hijacked American Airlines passenger plane piloted by Mohamed Atta slammed into the north tower of New York City's World Trade Center. Within twenty minutes, a second hijacked United Airlines plane piloted by Marwan al-Shehhi struck the south tower. At 9:45 a.m., another hijacked plane crashed into the western façade of the Pentagon, and less than a half hour later, a fourth hijacked plane plummeted to the earth in a wooded field outside Somerset, Pennsylvania. At 9:50 a.m., the south tower of the World Trade Center began to collapse, each floor pancaking onto the one below. Forty minutes later, the north tower seemed to implode. The collapse of the Twin Towers sent dust and smoke billowing through the streets of Lower Manhattan as thousands of terrified New Yorkers ran for cover. Initial estimates put the number of dead from this terrorist attack at over 5,000, but later the death toll was determined to be 2,974.

Suppose someone were to maintain that 9/11 was justified because of its consequences. If we were consequentialists, we couldn't just dismiss such a claim out of hand. We would have to determine what benefits bin Laden, al-Qaeda, and their supporters could be reasonably expected to derive from 9/11, and we would have to look at other consequences too.

So what were the consequences of 9/11? First, there was the U.S.-led military intervention in Afghanistan. Surely, bin Laden had expected that intervention. However, he probably thought U.S.-led forces would get bogged down in a ground war in Afghanistan just the way the Russians had in the 1980s, and to some degree that has proven to be the case. And even though he was eventually killed by U.S. special forces near the capital of Pakistan in 2011, bin Laden, al-Qaeda, and their supporters might still have benefited from this intervention overall.

Needless to say, what is not in doubt is that the main benefit of 9/11 for bin Laden and his supporters came about in a way that he most assuredly could have only hoped for: through the U.S. invasion and occupation of Iraq. The cost of that military intervention for the United States to date has been more than 6,000 dead, over 50,000 wounded, and a currently estimated financial cost of $4 trillion.[11] The financial cost of the war alone imposed a significant burden on the United States that surely limits its military options in the near future. The United States cannot now fight $4 trillion wars against al-Qaeda-inspired insurrections elsewhere in the Middle East. This limitation on what the United States can now do, resulting from its invasion and occupation of Iraq, therefore, converts into a benefit for bin Laden and his supporters. This is because bin Laden's overall goal was to limit and diminish U.S. power, particularly in the Middle East.

So does this mean that 9/11 was justified on consequentialist grounds because of the reasonably expected or hoped for benefits that bin Laden and his supporters derived from it? Does this also mean that acts of torture as practiced by the United States with British support were justified on consequentialist grounds because of the benefits that the United States and its allies reasonably expected or hoped to derive therefrom? Not necessarily. Among other things, this is because consequentialism requires that all, not just some, of the consequences of an action be taken into account in assessing its justification. So we need to consider the harms that could have been reasonably expected to derive from these actions as well as their benefits.

Here it is important to note that consequentialism has to be evaluating our actions in terms of the consequences we either reasonably expected or hoped to bring about or in terms of the actual consequences of our actions that we reasonably expected or hoped to bring about. This is because the morality of our actions cannot be determined by any actual consequences of our actions that we could not have reasonably expected and hence were unknowable to us, such as some consequence our actions might have a hundred years from now.

So while we sometimes talk about actions as being justified or unjustified in terms of their actual consequences, the usual presumption when we make such claims is that the actual consequences of the actions either were reasonably expected or could have been reasonably expected by the agents who brought them about. Of course, we might reasonably expect that we are going to bring about some consequence or other and something totally unexpected happens. But then we normally cannot be morally blamed or praised for bringing about such unexpected consequences.[12]

Even so, we do seem to be able to find cases where the irreparable harm we knowingly inflict on some appears to be outweighed by the overall expected benefit to others. Surely, Cheney thought that the acts of torture inflicted on detainees by the CIA were justified by their good consequences for others. And just as surely, bin Laden thought that the deaths and destruction of 9/11 were justified by their good consequences, particularly in the Middle East.[13] Nevertheless, according to consequentialist ethics, whether such acts of torture or terror were justified depends on whether the significant harms inflicted on some are, in fact, outweighed by greater benefits to others.

Hypothetical examples

To better illustrate the possibility of justifying inflicting significant harms on some for the sake of greater benefit to others, philosophers have frequently proposed using hypothetical examples where, unlike in real-life examples, all the relevant facts that characterize the examples can be definitively specified by just stipulating them to be thus and so.

Consider the following example. A talented transplant surgeon happens to have five patients; two need lung transplants while the other three need heart, liver, and kidney transplants, respectively. Each of them will die shortly without the needed transplant. Unfortunately, at the present moment, there are no organs from legitimate sources available to perform any of these transplant operations. However, a healthy young male, who just happened to be passing through, comes to see the doctor for a routine checkup. In the course of the checkup, with speedy lab work, the doctor is able to discover that the young man's organs are compatible with all five of her dying patients. Suppose, further, that the young male happens to have no surviving relatives or close friends so that if he were to disappear, no one would suspect anything untoward had happened. So would there not be good consequentialist grounds for carving up the young male and transplanting his organs to save the five terminal patients?

Consider also the following example.[14] A large person who is leading a party of spelunkers[15] gets himself stuck in the mouth of a cave in which floodwaters are rising quickly. The trapped party of spelunkers just happen to have a stick of dynamite with which they can blast the person out of the mouth of the cave. Imagine the large person's head is inside the cave, so either the spelunkers use the dynamite to blast him out of the mouth of the cave or they all drown, the person with them. In this example, it is difficult to deny the moral permissibility of dynamiting the person out of the mouth of the cave. After all, if that were not done, the whole party of spelunkers would die, the large person included. So the sacrifice that would be imposed on the large person in this example would not be that great.

Now suppose the large person's head is outside rather

than inside the cave. Under these circumstances, the large person would not die when the other spelunkers drown. Presumably after slimming down just a bit, he would eventually squeeze his way out of the mouth of the cave. In this example, could the party of spelunkers trapped in the cave still legitimately use the stick of dynamite they have to save themselves by blasting the large person out of the mouth of the cave?

This version of the spelunker example is very similar to the other examples we have been considering – they all involve imposing irreparable suffering or death on some in order to provide a greater benefit to others. Cheney supported torturing detainees in order to provide greater benefits to others. Osama bin Laden surely thought that the death and destruction of 9/11 were justified because of the benefits they produced, particularly in the Middle East. Similarly, our hypothetical surgeon wanted to save the lives of five of her terminally ill patients by carving up one perfectly healthy young man. So does consequentialism approve of these actions? If it does, is there any reason to object to consequentialism interpreted in this way?

An objection to consequentialist ethics: never do evil

Now it is sometimes thought that what is morally objectionable about consequentialism is that it conflicts with the principle "Never do evil that good may come of it." This principle, which is sometimes called the Pauline principle because it is found in the writings of St. Paul, has long been a mainstay in ethics. Applied to the surgeon case, the Pauline principle clearly prohibits our hypothetical surgeon's carving up one perfectly healthy young person to save the lives of five of her terminally ill patients. That would surely be a prohibited case of doing evil that good may come of it.

Nevertheless, there are also exceptions to the Pauline principle that any defensible moral theory must recognize. Suppose, for example, that the only way a doctor can get out of a crowded subway to attend to an emergency is by stepping on a few people's toes. Surely, the harm that the doctor inflicts on those innocent individuals whose toes he steps upon would be justified in any defensible moral theory by the greater benefit he would be able to accomplish in the emergency situation. In this example, the harm inflicted for the sake of the greater benefit is trivial. In other examples, however, the harm inflicted is not trivial, but it is still reparable, as when one might lie to a temporarily depressed friend to keep her from committing suicide – an act for which she will be profusely grateful later. So here, too, any defensible moral theory would hold that the harm inflicted on an innocent person in this example is justified by the greater benefit that results.

Yet what about examples where the harm inflicted is neither trivial nor reparable? Most of our earlier examples were of this sort: Cheney's use of torture, bin Laden's use of terror, the surgeon's harvesting the healthy man's organs, and the spelunkers' use of the large person. For such examples, we could always imagine significant benefits accruing to a large number of people (e.g., one hundred, one thousand, one million, whatever number you want) that would be lost unless one particular (innocent) individual were seriously harmed or killed. Surely, at some point, any defensible moral theory will allow such sacrifices. So what is morally wrong with consequentialism, if anything, cannot be that it justifies doing harm to innocents in order to secure a greater benefit for others. As we just noted, any defensible moral theory will have to do that to some extent. Rather, what must be morally wrong with consequentialism, if it is a truly objectionable moral theory, must be that it permits or requires harms of this sort when the trade-offs cannot be justified, or, put another way, what must be wrong with consequentialism, if it is a truly objectionable moral theory, is that it permits or requires too many exceptions to the Pauline principle.

Refining the objection: necessary harm and independent reasons

So when are such trade-offs not justified? Surely, they are not justified when the same benefits could be secured in some other feasible way that would result in less harm. To be morally justified, the harm inflicted must be a necessary means for achieving the good results.

Of course, in a hypothetically specified example like the large person stuck in the mouth of the cave, we can just stipulate that the good results could not have been achieved in any other way and so force the conclusion that dynamiting the large person out of the mouth of the cave is the only way of securing the desired result. In real-life examples, however, this condition is often not met.

Consider our earlier examples. Cheney maintained that the torture of detainees was necessary to obtain important information, but the FBI, who questioned some of the same detainees, maintained that the really important information that had been gotten from these detainees had been elicited beforehand, without the use of torture.[16] So it is far from clear that torture was a necessary means for achieving the good results that Cheney sought, as would be required if torture were to be justified by consequentialism. Similarly, it appears that bin Laden could have achieved the same good results he sought – lessening of U.S. power in the Middle East – without using terror, that is, without directly attacking nonmilitary targets. For example, suppose that instead of targeting the Twin Towers, he had targeted two of the U.S. military academies and the Pentagon. Surely the Bush administration would most likely have responded pretty much the same way it did, leading to the same costly war in Iraq that has lessened the ability of the United States to project its power in the Middle East. Nor were the deaths of the noncombatants onboard the hijacked planes necessary to attain bin Laden's political goal. If cargo planes had been hijacked instead and their pilots had parachuted to safety, bin Laden's political goal might even have been better achieved. So here too it is far from clear that bin Laden's acts of terror on 9/11 were a necessary means for achieving the good results he wanted, as would be required if those acts were to be justified by consequentialism.

As we noted in the crises faced by the surgeon and the trapped group of spelunkers, hypothetical examples can be specified so that their good consequences can be realized only by the proposed means. Real-life examples are rarely so simple. For instance, we can easily think of human organ transplant schemes that don't require the sacrifice of innocent people's lives. Most, if not all, human organ transplant needs could be met if there were laws that required that after people, or maybe just accident victims, died, their organs were made available for possible transplants through some equitable distribution system. So for the most part, at least in real-life cases, the proposed harmful means would not be necessary for achieving the desired goals.

In the final analysis, we cannot easily justify imposing irreparable harm on some to achieve greater benefit to others by appealing to a consequentialist moral theory when the harms and benefits have not been appropriately specified. This is also particularly true in real-life circumstances, where there almost always seem to be alternative ways of achieving the desired consequences that avoid the irreparable harm – alternatives that would be favored by consequentialism. What this shows is that consequentialism is clearly far less objectionable than some have claimed. When all the alternatives are taken into account, especially in real-life cases, it is not very likely that the view will, in fact, justify imposing irreparable harm on some innocent individuals in order to secure greater benefit for others.

Nevertheless, we would like to have stronger grounds for saying that consequentialism would not justify such impositions other than by claiming that as a *matter of fact* they would not be needed to maximize good consequences. The Pauline principle, even when it is recognized that there are justified exceptions to it, still seems to have normative force against consequentialism in certain cases, such as the case of a hypothetical surgeon's carving up one perfectly healthy young person to save the lives of five of her terminally ill patients. So we still need to find some way of reconciling consequentialism in a wide range of cases with the Pauline principle's requirement never to do evil that good may come of it. As we shall see in the next chapter, this is also the only way we would be able to reconcile consequentialist theories of ethics with nonconsequentialist theories of ethics given the latter all impose significant constraints on the pursuit of good consequences.

4

Nonconsequentialism

Nonconsequentialism, like consequentialism, agrees with the defender of morality in Chapter 2, but it differs from consequentialism by imposing constraints on the pursuit of overall good consequences.

Now one way to think about nonconsequentialism is captured by the following challenge: *What if everyone did that?* For example, suppose you are considering cheating on your taxes, evading military service, or telling a small lie to advance your projects. How would you respond if challenged with the question, "What if everyone did that?"

Notice that the challenge is not that everyone else will definitely act as you are proposing to act, and so the results of the combined acts of you and others would be disastrous. That would be a different argument – one based on the actual consequences of your actions and the actions of others – and it would not be a good argument because there is no reason to think that your action would be accompanied or followed by everyone else acting in exactly the same way. Fortunately, that is not the argument that is being offered here. The argument that is being offered here is based not on what actually happens but rather on what would happen if others did act as you are proposing to act.

Kantian nonconsequentialism

Arguments of this sort trace back to the work of Immanuel Kant. Born in Konigsberg, East Prussia (now called Kaliningrad, and part of Russia), Kant is said to have never journeyed more than forty miles from the city. He was also so methodical that, according to legend, the citizens of Konigsberg were said to set their watches to his daily 3 p.m. walks. His most important works in ethics are *Foundations of a Metaphysics of Morals* (1786), *Critique of Practical Reason* (1790), and *Metaphysics of Morals* (1797).

Kant's Categorical Imperative test

Now, according to Kant, for our actions to be moral, they must be able to satisfy a certain test – a test that is somewhat similar to asking, "What if everyone did that?" Kant called his test the *Categorical Imperative*, and as he first formulates the test, it tells us to: "Act only on that maxim which you can at the same time will to be a universal law."[1] To apply this test, when you are contemplating performing a particular act, you have to ask what rule you would be proposing to follow if you were to perform that act. This is the "maxim of the act." Kant gives the following example to help explain how his test works:

> Suppose I need to borrow money, and I know that no one will lend it to me unless I promise to repay the loan. But suppose I also know that I will not be able to repay. Should I therefore promise to repay the loan knowing that I will not be able to do so in order to persuade someone to loan the money to me?[2]

If I were to do that, the "maxim of my act" (the rule I would be following) would be: Whenever you need a loan, promise to repay it, regardless of whether you believe you actually will be able to repay it.

Could this rule become a universal law? Not if, as we are assuming to be the case, everyone would know that, under these circumstances, people's promises are worthless. Because then no one would believe such promises. So no one would make loans on the basis of them. As Kant puts it, "No one would believe what was promised to him but would only laugh at any such assertion as vain pretense."[3] So it would not be possible for a practice of lying promises to be sustained under such circumstances. As Kant sees it, making lying promises under such circumstances cannot satisfy his Categorical Imperative test.

Using another example, Kant explains his test as follows: "Suppose someone refused to help others in need, saying to herself, 'What concern of mine is it? Let each one be happy as heaven wills . . . but to his welfare or to his assistance in time of need I have no desire to contribute.'"[4] Again, Kant maintains this rule cannot be willed to be a universal law. For he thinks that at some time in the future this person will surely find herself to be in need of assistance from others, and then she would not want others to be unconcerned about her. So, according to Kant, her commitment now not to help others in need would put her in conflict with what she would will later, assuming that she finds herself to be in need.

Kant, egoism, and hypothetical imperatives

Kant also believes that following maxims sanctioned by his Categorical Imperative test is a requirement of rationality as well as morality. However, egoists who are clearly opposed to morality can also be understood as acting according to a universal law, although it is a different universal law from the one followed by those committed to morality. For egoists, the appropriate law is, *Everyone ought to do what best serves his or her own self-interest.* This principle seems in every way as ultimate and law-like as the Categorical Imperative and the maxims that satisfy its test.[5]

What distinguishes the requirements of egoism, however, is their failure to pass Kant's Categorical Imperative test. While the egoist allows that others ought to do whatever best serves their own self-interest, she need not want or will that others do so, especially when that conflicts with what best serves the egoist's own self-interest. Viewed in this way, there is nothing irrational about this behavior. In fact, as we noted in Chapter 2, this behavior parallels that of players in competitive games. In baseball, for example, a pitcher may think that the runner at first base ought to steal second while not wanting her to do so and indeed hoping to foil any attempt the runner makes. Since we do not regard the pitcher's behavior as irrational, no reason has been given for thinking that analogous behavior of the egoist is, in fact, irrational.

The egoist, however, would have no problem at all endorsing Kant's account of hypothetical imperatives. For Kant, hypothetical imperatives tell us what we ought to do provided we have the relevant desires. If you want a career in ballet, then you ought to commit yourself to practicing long hours. If you want to qualify for the Boston Marathon, then you ought to be running over ten miles a day. The egoist has no problem at all accepting the conditional force of such hypothetical imperatives given that they in no way conflict with the normative commitments of being an egoist. This is because you can always reject the relevant desires on which the normative force of the hypothetical imperatives depends. For example, if you no longer want a career in ballet, but now you want one in engineering, certain hypothetical imperatives lose their normative force for you, while others acquire such force for you. Moreover, accepting the conditional normative force of certain hypothetical imperatives is perfectly consistent with rejecting the Categorical Imperative test as a requirement of rationality. The egoist, committed to her own way of universalizing, is not shown to be irrational because she is not committed to universalizing as Kant's Categorical Imperative test requires.[6] Hence, if one wants to defeat the egoist on grounds of rationality, one needs to utilize the approach taken in Chapter 2.

A central requirement of morality

Still, meeting Kant's test does capture a central requirement of morality: its universalizability. What is morally required for me to do must be morally required for anyone else who is relevantly similar to me and who is in relevantly similar circumstances as well. Even so, maxims can satisfy Kant's test and still be morally defective. To see this, consider a variant of Kant's lying promise example where the person's maxim is to make lying promises, but only when a sufficient number of other people, similarly situated, are not doing the same. Restricted in this manner, the universalizing of one's lying would not negatively affect the general practice of promising because only a restricted number of people would be breaking their promises. Such a maxim would then pass Kant's Categorical Imperative test.

Universalizability is not enough

However, there is a moral problem with such maxims. They go too far in allowing just anyone to break a promise provided a sufficient number of other people are not doing the same. While exceptions to promise-keeping surely cannot be so numerous that they would have a negative impact on the practice, not having such an impact, as required by Kant's Categorical Imperative test, is not sufficient to justify making an exception of oneself. Morality requires more; it requires that promise-breaking not impose unreasonable burdens on others and so it must be further limited to just those cases where people have the best reasons for breaking their promises. Simply claiming that my breaking my promises in a limited way, and others doing the same, would not have a negative impact on the practice of promise-making does not provide a sufficient justification for my promise-breaking. There must be some additional reason that justifies my promise-breaking, but not the promise-breaking of others who are similarly situated. Morality requires that the universalizability of maxims be combined with adequate moral grounds for determining when exceptions are to be explicitly or implicitly included in those maxims.

Furthermore, the maxims that people employ in such cases could never be fully specified. Obviously, the laws of a nation can never be fully specified to indicate all the present and future exceptions its members should make to them. That is why we need courts to interpret such laws. But the same holds for the promises and other agreements we make. They, too, can never be fully specified to indicate all the present and future exceptions we should be making to them. In general, it is universalizability together with appropriate grounds for making exceptions that determines the morality that binds us in this regard.

Yet, just as Kant's Categorical Imperative universalizability test needs to be supplemented with adequate moral grounds for exceptions in order to properly capture what we are morally required to do, something similar holds of the "What if everyone did that?" argument. It is not, all by itself, a sufficient moral test. The argument rightly indicates that moral requirements must be universalizable, and it further suggests that your act would not be justified when everyone's acting as you are acting would lead to very bad consequences. The reason for this is not that these bad consequences would actually happen. Rather, it is that in acting in this way, you would be able to reap the benefits of your promise-breaking only because a sufficient number of other people, similarly situated, did not act as you did. What this shows is that without some reason justifying your promise-breaking, but not theirs, your act of promise-breaking would not be morally justified because it would impose an unreasonable burden on others and thereby give you an unfair advantage.

Other formulations of Kant's test

Not surprisingly, in two of his other formulations of the Categorical Imperative, Kant explicitly introduces further moral constraints on his universalizability test. In one formulation, Kant tells us to not treat people only as a means. He applies this formulation of his Categorical Imperative to his example of someone who wants to make a lying promise, claiming that to make such a promise treats the person to whom the promise is made simply as a means. Yet, as we noted, if certain exceptions to keeping one's promises can be morally justified, then presumably doing so would involve showing appropriative regard to everyone affected and so not involve treating anyone simply as a means.

Kant also thinks that people are used simply as a means when "attempts on the freedom and property of others" are made.[7] While he does not make it clear when he thinks this occurs, contemporary libertarians often claim to be following him because of the importance they place on liberty and property.

In still another formulation of his Categorical Imperative, Kant also requires that our universalized maxims must be acceptable to everyone in an idealized "kingdom of ends," where all are treated respectfully. Prominent 20th-century philosopher John Rawls and his followers have worked to develop the normative standard suggested by this formulation of Kant's Categorical Imperative, but they have done so in a way that appears to conflict with a libertarian interpretation of Kantian ethics.

Thus, the moral constraints found in these other formulations of Kant's Categorical Imperative test do help to rule out problematic exceptions to universal practices that unfairly disadvantage some to benefit others. Unfortunately, they also imply seemingly divergent interpretations of Kantian ethics concerning how we should treat the poor or disadvantaged that require a resolution in order for Kantian ethics to be of much practical use. So we will need to consider each of these interpretations. One interpretation endorses a welfare liberal (welfare and beyond) perspective with respect to the poor or disadvantaged, while the other endorses a libertarian (no welfare) perspective.

Clearly there is a need to reconcile these two Kantian perspectives, as we will attempt to do in the next chapter. But first we need to consider the other main form of nonconsequentialism that has its historical roots in ancient Greece, particularly in the work of Aristotle (384–322 BCE). As it turns out, Aristotelian ethics also gives rise to two interpretations of how we should treat the poor or disadvantaged: one that endorses a welfare liberal (welfare and beyond) perspective with respect to the poor or disadvantaged, the other endorsing a libertarian (no welfare) perspective.

Aristotelian nonconsequentialism

Born in the northern Greek city of Stagira in Macedonia, Aristotle entered Plato's Academy when he was eighteen and studied and taught there for approximately twenty years. Plato is said to have considered him "the mind" of the Academy. Nevertheless, in his will, Plato named his nephew Speusippus head of the Academy rather than his gifted student Aristotle. So Aristotle left Athens and went to Assos in Asia Minor, where he established a branch campus of the Academy. In 343 BCE, Philip of Macedon invited Aristotle to tutor his thirteen-year-old son, Alexander, who was to become Alexander the Great. Soon after the death of Philip, Aristotle returned to Athens and began his own school, the Lyceum, where he produced most of the works that survive to this day in the form of lecture notes.

Happiness and the virtuous life

In one of his most famous works, the *Nicomachean Ethics*, named after his son, who is supposed to have edited it, Aristotle attempts to provide ethics with a secure foundation. He begins by noting that all human activity aims at some good. He argues that, for humans, happiness is the ultimate good, but that happiness is wrongly thought to consist simply in pleasure, wealth, and honor. Rightly understood, Aristotle argues that happiness for humans requires a virtuous life. So the proper goal for humans is to be virtuous. Thus, ethics is primarily seen as a way of *being* rather than as a way of *acting*, although the two are obviously connected since being virtuous will require acting in certain ways on certain occasions.

For Aristotle, a virtue is a desirable trait of character that is a mean between two vices, one of excess and the other of deficiency. Courage, for example, is understood to be a mean between the vices of foolhardiness and cowardice. Aristotle also distinguishes between intellectual and moral virtues. Intellectual virtues, like logic and mathematics, can be taught. By contrast, moral virtues, such as benevolence, honesty, loyalty, and patience, can

be only learned through practice. As Aristotle puts it,
"[M]en become builders by building and lyre-players
by playing the lyre; so too we become just by doing just
acts, temperate by doing temperate acts, brave by doing
brave acts."[8]

Aristotle uses the virtue of courage to further illustrate
how a moral virtue is a mean between two vices, one
of excess and the other of deficiency. Courage, when
considered more closely, has two components: fear and
confidence. As a consequence, we can err in regard to
either factor by having too much or too little fear, or too
much or too little confidence. If we have too little fear or
too much confidence, we display the vice of foolhardiness. If we have too much fear or too little confidence,
we display the opposing vice of cowardice.

Nevertheless, Aristotle thinks that his analysis of
virtue doesn't work for all cases. To show this, he gives
the example of murder as an action that is always wrong
and does not admit of a mean. But regarding murder as
always wrong does not seem to conflict with Aristotle's
analysis of virtue because the relevant virtue here, which
is a mean, can be called respect for the lives of others.
Murder then would be one way of displaying the vice of
too little respect for the lives of others. The contrasting
vice would be that of showing too much respect for the
lives of others. This would involve being unduly willing
to sacrifice one's own life for others, especially when
such sacrifice is not really needed or deserved. As further
support for Aristotle's analysis, we might also think of
virtue generally as a mean between favoring our own
interests too much or too little or as a mean between
favoring the interests of others too much or too little.[9]

It was also part of Aristotle's view that people's ability to be virtuous is vastly unequal. As Aristotle saw it,
some men were natural slaves while all women lacked
the full capacity to reason. As a consequence, both
groups were destined by nature to be ruled by free men.
Happily, contemporary Aristotelians, benefiting from

further reflection on the relevant data, have chosen not to follow Aristotle in this respect.

Characterizing the virtuous life

Nevertheless, it is not easy to properly characterize a virtuous life. Contemporary philosopher Alasdair MacIntyre attempts to characterize it in terms of practices that have goods that are internal as opposed to external to them.[10] In soccer, for example, a good internal to the practice would be the pleasure that comes from coordinated play with your teammates, while a good external to the practice would be the cheering you happen to receive from those watching you play. Yet while MacIntyre's connection of a virtuous life to practices is helpful, he does not go on to determine which practices constitute a virtuous life, and unfortunately this leaves the concept of a virtuous life open to a multitude of different and possibly conflicting interpretations.

Another contemporary philosopher, Martha Nussbaum, tries to do better. She defines virtue as being disposed to respond well in the eight important spheres of shared human experience, which are as follows:[11]

- mortality,
- the body,
- pleasure and pain,
- cognitive ability,
- practical reason,
- early infant development,
- affiliation,
- and humor.

With respect to each of these spheres, Nussbaum claims that relevant virtues can be specified in an objective and nonrelativist way. While this does add more detail to an account of a virtuous life, it still leaves many questions unanswered. In particular, it leaves open the question of whether a virtuous concern with these spheres of human experience is just centered on one's own good (happiness) or whether it also takes into account the good (happiness) of others. Now Aristotle's linkage of the virtuous life with one's own happiness might seem to favor the first interpretation. Yet some contemporary Aristotelians, notably Julia Annas and Robert Adams, favor an account of a virtuous life that includes a strong concern for the good of others as well as for one's own good.[12] Such an interpretation would also make the view more similar to Kantian and consequentialist ethics, both of which have a strong other-regarding focus. In turn, such an interpretation should lead to consideration of distant peoples and future generations within Aristotelian ethics, given that these other-regarding concerns are also taken up in Kantian and consequentialist ethics.

Conflicts with Kantian ethics

Another area of conflict between Aristotelians and Kantians has been over the importance of rules to morality. Some Aristotelians have noted how difficult it is to determine relevant rules with respect to many of the virtues of ordinary life.[13] Consider the virtues of gratitude and self-respect. It is difficult to know how we could specify rules relevant to these virtues except by using the uninformative admonitions "Be grateful" and "Respect oneself." We surely cannot determine what is required in such a way, for example, that an ungrateful person could still obey the relevant rule with respect to gratitude while lacking the appropriate motives and beliefs required for exercising that virtue. Obeying rules of this sort requires having certain relevant intentions and beliefs which are not easy to specify. So, for many of the virtues of ordinary life, it turns out that rules are not very useful for communicating what should be done. What are generally more helpful to communicating what should be done are stories or paradigm cases of virtuous action, such as the parable of the Good Samaritan.

Now while it is usually Aristotelians who make these points about the limitations of rules, it is not clear why Kantians or consequentialists need deny anything that Aristotelians are claiming here. Kantians and consequentialists can grant that with respect to many of the virtues of ordinary life, there is no corresponding rule that is useful in communicating what should be done. At the same time, Kantians and consequentialists can point out that with respect to other virtues of ordinary life, there are more useful and more informative rules. For instance, for truthfulness, "Don't lie," for honesty, "Don't steal," and for respect for innocent life, "Don't kill." The reason these rules are a bit more useful and more informative is that they provide an alternative way of characterizing what their respective virtues require. However, Aristotelians need not deny that this is the case, and this should lead to considerable agreement between Kantians and Aristotelians concerning both the limitations and the usefulness of moral rules.[14]

Focusing on how we should act

While Aristotelian ethics is celebrated for its focus on character and intentions (how we should be) rather than actions (how we should act), contemporary philosopher Rosalind Hursthouse has sought to show that Aristotelian ethics can still tell us how we should act. For Hursthouse, right action is what a virtuous agent would do in the circumstances.[15] Sometimes this standard is interpreted to require doing what a perfectly virtuous agent – say, Jesus, Buddha, or Muhammad – would do in the circumstances. Yet this may not be the best way to interpret the standard because it may be impossible for a perfectly virtuous agent to actually be in the particular circumstances in which we find ourselves.

More usefully, Aristotle compares the process through which someone learns to be virtuous to the process by which a person learns to play a harp.[16] At each stage, what a person should do is not what a completely virtuous person (or fully expert harpist) does, but rather what a person at that particular stage of development should do next to become more virtuous (or a better harpist). In the pursuit of virtue, the stage a person is presently at could, for example, involve a grossly immoral lifestyle, and so it would not make sense to ask what a perfectly virtuous agent would do in such circumstances because, of course, a perfectly virtuous agent would never be in such circumstances. In fact, no virtuous agent would ever be in just those circumstances. Still, if you happen to find yourself in such circumstances, you can just ask yourself what would be the next step you should take to morally improve your character.

The priority question

Now consider circumstances that are compatible with the existence of a morally virtuous agent. For such circumstances, do the choices of morally virtuous agents actually determine the rightness of acts? Consider an act of saving a child from drowning. Isn't the fundamental reason this act is right that it would save the child's life, rather than that a morally virtuous agent (with the requisite life-saving abilities) would choose to perform that act? If anything, it is the rightness of the act that would seem to explain why a morally virtuous person would choose to perform it.

Does this imply that consequentialist and Kantian ethics, with their focus on ethics as a way of acting, have an advantage over Aristotelian ethics, with its focus on ethics as a way of being? Not necessarily. There are other examples where the rightness or wrongness of an action is far less clear and for which the best way to determine what to do is to consider what an ideally virtuous person, such as Socrates, Joan of Arc, Martin Luther King, Jr., or even your own uncle Phil or aunt Natasha, would do in such circumstances.

For example, imagine you are trying to decide what to do with your life. Surely, considering what ideally a virtuous agent with your abilities would choose to do can help you answer this question. Even consequentialists and Kantians recognize the usefulness of appealing to what ideally virtuous agents would choose to do when determining what is right and wrong. For example, consequentialist ethics appeals to what an ideally sympathetic agent would choose to do and Kantian ethics appeals to what ideally rational people in the kingdom of ends would choose to do. It would seem best, therefore, not to assign a conclusive priority to any of the three ethical perspectives in this regard.

Ayn Rand's Aristotelian ethics

However, there is another popular version of Aristotelian ethics that seems strongly opposed to most contemporary interpretations of Kantian and consequentialist ethics, and so would be against any kind of practical reconciliation with those views. This interpretation is found in the work of modern novelist/philosopher Ayn Rand (1905–82). Given that her work provides us with an interpretation of Aristotelian ethics that is strongly opposed to most contemporary interpretations of both Kantian and consequentialist ethics, it clearly deserves our attention.

Ayn Rand (Alice Rosenbaum) was born in St. Petersburg, Russia. Her most successful novels were *The Fountainhead* (1943), which was made into a movie starring Gary Cooper and Patricia Neal, and *Atlas Shrugged* (1957), both of which books have sold millions of copies. Rand also published a number of works of nonfiction, such as *The Virtue of Selfishness* (1964), in which she more directly set out her version of Aristotelian ethics.

Regarding Aristotle as the greatest of all philosophers, Rand draws on his view to develop a virtue theory of selfishness in which the primary moral requirement is to be simply concerned with one's own interests. She views her theory as opposed to an altruism that regards any action done for the benefit of others as good and any action done for one's own benefit as evil.[17] According to Rand,

> [E]very human being is an end in himself, not the means to the ends or welfare of others and, therefore, that man must live for his own sake, neither sacrificing himself to others, nor sacrificing others to himself. To live for his own sake means that the achievement of his own happiness is man's highest moral purpose.[18]

Unfortunately, Rand's characterization of altruism here misses the mark as a critique of consequentialist and Kantian ethics. Neither of these views regards any action done for one's own benefit as evil. Rather, both views simply maintain that concern for one's own good (self-interest) is sometimes morally outweighed by concern for the good of others (altruism), occasionally even to the point of *requiring* the sacrifice or restriction of one's own good for the good of others.

Fortunately, Rand's critique of consequentialist and Kantian ethics does not depend on interpreting altruism as being radically opposed to self-interest. Her main argument can still be advanced against the moderate form of altruism that is actually endorsed by consequentialist and Kantian ethics. We can see this by looking at a speech that is given in *The Fountainhead* by Howard Roark, who represents Rand's ideal of a self-interested man.[19] At the end of the novel, when Roark gives this speech, he is on trial for dynamiting a building project that he had designed. Roark had secretly agreed to provide the architectural design for the project to its official architect, Peter Keating, without any monetary compensation, but only on the condition that his design not be altered in any way. Keating needed Roark's help with respect to the project because only Roark knew how to design it so as to provide sufficient low-income housing within the budgetary constraints. As the project was being built, however, Keating succumbed to pressure from others to alter its design in ways that destroyed the aesthetic unity that Roark had given it. So as the project was nearing completion, Roark, aided by Dominique Francon, who represented Rand's ideal of a self-interested woman in-the-making, blew the building up. At his trial, which was the climax of the novel, Roark offered the following defense for his action, which secured for him an acquittal:

> It is said that I have destroyed the home of the destitute. It is forgotten that but for me the destitute could not have had this particular home. Those who were concerned with the poor had to come to me, who have never been concerned, in order to help the poor. It is believed that the poverty of the future tenants gave them a right to my work. That their need constituted a claim on my life. That it was my duty to contribute anything demanded of me. . . . I came here to say that I do not recognize anyone's right to one minute of my life. Nor to any part of my energy. Nor to any achievement of mine. No matter who makes the claim, how large their number, or how great their need.[20]

Notice that although Roark does reject altruism in his speech, he can be seen to be rejecting even the moderate form of altruism actually endorsed by Kantian and consequentialist ethics and not just the extreme form of altruism that Rand claims to be against. So it makes more sense to make the real target of Rand's argument

the moderate form of altruism that both consequentialist and Kantian ethics actually endorse.

The No-Duty thesis

Now the main challenge Rand presents to other theories
of ethics is her No-Duty thesis, according to which we
have no duty to help the poor when we are rich or
talented.

Rand considers and rejects the possibility of such a
duty to help the poor arising in what she calls emergencies. For Rand, an emergency is "an unchosen,
unexpected event, limited in time, that creates conditions under which human survival is impossible, such as
a flood or earthquake."[21] For such emergencies, Rand
claims, "any help [we] give [to others] is an exception,
not a rule, an act of generosity, not a moral duty, that
it is marginal and incidental – as disasters are marginal
and incidental in the course of human existence."[22] Of
course, one could question whether the acts of generosity that Rand permits here are not grounded in the very
same altruism she rejects. Nevertheless, it is much more
important to question her rejection of a duty to help the
poor in such situations. That puts her view in conflict
with consequentialist theories generally and with at
least the welfare liberal interpretation of Kantian ethics.
So if we cannot find a way to reasonably resolve such
conflicts between consequentialist and nonconsequentialist theories, we will be in deep trouble. While other
sciences advance, ethics will remain with irresolvable
conflicts. Fortunately, the next chapter will provide the
reconciliation that is needed.

5

Reconciliation

To reconcile consequentialist and nonconsequentialist theories of ethics, at least at the practical level, we need to be able to do the following:

1 reconcile consequentialism with the Pauline principle requirement never to do evil that good may come of it, which is endorsed by nonconsequentialists;
2 reconcile libertarian interpretations of Kant's and Aristotle's ethics with alternative welfare liberal interpretations of those views; and
3 reconcile consequentialism, in general, with Kantian and Aristotelian ethics.

So let's examine each of these tasks in turn.

The first reconciliation

With regard to the first task, it is important to recognize that there are exceptions to the Pauline principle. For instance, doing evil that good may come of it is justified when the resulting evil or harm is:

1   trivial (e.g., as in the case of stepping on someone's foot to get out of a crowded subway);
2   easily reparable (e.g., as in the case of lying to a temporarily depressed friend to keep her from committing suicide); and, more significantly,
3   the only way to prevent far greater harm to innocent people (e.g., as in the case of shooting one of twenty civilian hostages to prevent, in the only way possible, the execution of all twenty).

No doubt, recognizing such exceptions to the Pauline principle does bring consequentialists and nonconsequentialists closer together. Nevertheless, if we are going to bring consequentialists and nonconsequentialists into full agreement with respect to the Pauline principle, we need to determine the extent of justifiable exemptions to that principle. This we can do by utilizing a fundamental principle of morality: the "Ought" implies "Can" principle.

Imagine that I were to fly through the air, like Superman, catch a small child as she is falling from her seventh-story apartment window, and restore her to the arms of her grateful parents. Surely that action, if I were to perform it, would be virtually guaranteed to maximize the good overall. Just the same, it is surely not something I am required to do, given that I clearly lack the physical powers of Superman to perform it. Similarly, what people ought to do has always been understood to be constrained by what they can or have the physical power to do. These constraints have been expressed by the "Ought" implies "Can" principle.

Traditionally, this principle has also been thought to extend not to just what we are physically capable of doing, but to what we are logically and psychologically capable of doing as well. Clearly, if an action is logically or psychologically impossible for us to do, then it can't be an action that we ought to do, any more than it would be the case for an action that is just physically impossible for us to do. Thus, the traditional "Ought" implies "Can" principle has always been accepted as a constraint on what we ought to do, and so a constraint on our doing evil to achieve good results. Let us now see how this principle can also be plausibly extended beyond its traditional reach.

Suppose you promised to attend a meeting on Friday, but on Thursday you're involved in a serious car accident, which leaves you in a coma. Surely it is no longer the case that you ought to attend the meeting now that you lack the power and thus are physically incapable of doing so. *Here comes the extension.* Suppose instead that on Thursday you develop a severe case of pneumonia for which you are hospitalized. Although it would not, as in the previous case, be physically impossible for you to attend the meeting, surely you could legitimately claim that you *cannot* attend the meeting on the grounds that the risk to your health involved in attending is a sacrifice that in these circumstances it would be unreasonable to require you to bear.

Thus, if sacrifices that are unreasonable to require us to bear give us legitimate grounds for not being required to perform certain acts, as they are widely thought to do, then we have another type of limitation on what we ought to do, similar to the constraints of the traditional "Ought" implies "Can" principle. Indeed, it is so similar to those constraints that we standardly convey it, as in the previous example, by saying that we *cannot* do such acts, just as we standardly say we *cannot* do acts that are logically, psychologically, or physically impossible for us to do. Accordingly, we have good reason to bring both of these restrictions together under the following expanded "Ought" implies "Can" principle: People are not morally required to do either what they lack the power to do or what would involve so great a sacrifice or restriction that it would be unreasonable to require them to perform such an action.

Now notice what happens when we apply this

principle to our hypothetical case of the surgeon harvesting a healthy young man's organs to save five terminally
ill patients. In this case, the young man in no way caused
the terminal illnesses of the five patients, and thus he is in
no way responsible for them. Nor are a large number of
lives at stake in this case. Rather, if the surgeon has her
way, the young man's life will be sacrificed to save the
lives of just five other people. While responsibility and
numbers are relevant factors for justifying exceptions in
such cases, in this particular case, neither of these factors justifies an exception. Of course, if our young man
were willing to volunteer to sacrifice his life to save the
five patients, that would make a difference. However, *I*
have just stipulated that the healthy man in our hypothetical case is *not* willing to volunteer. Accordingly, for
this case, an expanded "Ought" implies "Can" principle would reject the forceful harvesting of the young
man's organs as an unreasonable sacrifice, and hence
make it an action that morality cannot require, even if it
would maximize the good overall. Happily, this is just
the result we were looking for: a constraint on doing
evil to achieve good results that limits the imposition of
irreparable harm on innocent individuals.[1]

Nevertheless, although the expanded "Ought" implies
"Can" principle will generally reject the imposition of
irreparable harm on innocents to maximize the good
overall, it will not always do so. The few cases where
the principle will not reject such impositions will be
cases, similar to our spelunker example in Chapter 3,
where the imposition would be reasonable to require
anyone affected to accept. We can see how this is so
in the spelunker case because we can imagine all the
spelunkers, the large person included, hypothetically
agreeing beforehand that if one of them gets stuck in the
mouth of the cave, a stick of dynamite should be used
to blast that person out. That hypothetical agreement
serves to establish the reasonableness of the imposition
in this and in similar cases. Of course, in real-life cases,

the application of the expanded "Ought" implies "Can" principle can be difficult to determine, but probably no more difficult to determine than what would maximize the good overall in such cases.

The obvious advantage of using this expanded "Ought" implies "Can" principle to limit exceptions to the Pauline principle is that the principle is internal to consequentialist ethics itself. In fact, the principle is internal to all moral and political perspectives. The principle combines the traditional "Ought" implies "Can" principle with a linkage between reason and morality that understands that the requirements of morality cannot impose unreasonable sacrifices on people. Given that both of these constraints are endorsed by consequentialists and nonconsequentialists alike, their combination in this principle has to be endorsed as well. In this way, we have reached the first reconciliation we needed between consequentialism and nonconsequentialism.

The second reconciliation

We turn now to our second task of reconciliation. Can a libertarian interpretation of Kant's and Aristotle's ethics be reconciled with a welfare liberal interpretation of Kant's and Aristotle's ethics?

As we have noted, Kantian ethics is open to two interpretations. One endorses a welfare liberal (welfare and beyond) perspective with respect to the poor or disadvantaged, while the other interpretation endorses a libertarian (no welfare) perspective. Likewise, Ayn Rand gives Aristotelian ethics a libertarian interpretation, while other Aristotelians, such as Julia Annas and Robert Adams, favor a welfare liberal interpretation. So we need to determine whether these interpretations can be reconciled at least in practice.

Now John Rawls is clearly the best-known defender of the welfare liberal perspective. In his widely acclaimed book *A Theory of Justice*, Rawls argues that moral or just principles would emerge from an idealized choice situation – analogous to Kant's "kingdom of ends," where everyone is respected as an end in him- or herself and not simply as a means.[2] Yet Rawls goes beyond Kant by interpreting the conditions of his idealized choice situation to explicitly require a "veil of ignorance." This veil of ignorance, Rawls claims, requires that we discount certain knowledge about ourselves in order to reach fair agreements.

A good example of what is at issue here is the practice of withholding information from juries. As we know, judges sometimes refuse to allow juries to hear certain testimony. The rationale behind this practice is that certain information is highly prejudicial or irrelevant to the case at hand. The hope is that without this information, juries will be more likely to reach fair verdicts. Similarly, when prejudicial or irrelevant information is blurted out in the courtroom, intentionally or unintentionally, judges will usually instruct juries to discount that information, hoping to increase the likelihood that juries will reach fair verdicts. Of course, whether judges and juries in fact carry out their responsibilities in this regard is beside the point. What is crucial is that it is recognized in these contexts that justice demands that we discount certain information in order to achieve just results.

Rawls's idealized choice situation can be seen as simply a generalization of this practice. It maintains that if we are to achieve a fair system of rights and duties in general, then we must discount certain information about ourselves when choosing our system of rights and duties. In particular, we must discount our knowledge of whether we are rich or poor, talented or untalented, male or female, or straight, gay, or bisexual. In general, this ideal of justice requires that we should choose as though we were standing behind an imaginary veil of ignorance with respect to most particular facts about ourselves, anything that would bias our choice or stand in the way of unanimous agreement. Rawls calls this choice situation "the original position" because it is the position we should start from when determining what fundamental rights and duties people should have.

It should be obvious that Rawls's original position is designed in such a way that it is virtually impossible for some kind of enforced welfare system not to be chosen. If Abigail is assuming that she doesn't know whether she is rich or poor, and she is deciding whether her society should have a tax-supported welfare system or not, surely she will want a welfare system. She would reason like this: If I turn out to be rich, I may be a bit unhappy that part of my wealth is taxed away to support the needy. But if I am poor and my society has no tax-supported welfare system, then without a considerable amount of charity, things could be very bad for me with my basic needs not being met. So choosing behind a veil of ignorance in Rawls's original position, everyone would favor a tax-supported welfare system of some sort.

Nor would the welfare system that would be chosen in Rawls's original position be unconditional. Recall Aesop's fable of the grasshopper and the ant. Throughout the summer, the grasshopper enjoyed himself, refusing to store up food for the coming winter, while the ant worked hard to do just that. With the approach of winter, the grasshopper pleaded with the ant for help but the ant refused, reminding the grasshopper that he had done nothing to store up food for himself when he had the chance to do so. Similarly, persons in Rawls's original position would favor making their tax-supported welfare system conditional on the poor first doing what they legitimately can do to help themselves. Even if they turned out to be in a position analogous to that of the grasshopper in Aesop's fable, persons in Rawls's original position would reason they would not be justified in forcefully requiring others to help them. Nevertheless, while one Kantian-inspired ethical view and one Aristotelian-inspired view are thus said to lead to a tax-supported welfare system, another Kantian-inspired ethical view and another Aristotelian-inspired view, reflecting different parts of Kant's and Aristotle's theories, are said to lead to a rejection of just such a system. We need to find some way to reconcile these views.

Libertarianism

Now, some contemporary libertarians see themselves as defenders of an ideal of liberty that has Kantian roots and avoids treating people as means only. F. A. Hayek, who received a Nobel Prize in economics, saw his work as restating an ideal of liberty for our times: "We are concerned with that condition of men in which coercion of some by others is reduced as much as possible in society."[3] Similarly, American philosopher and Libertarian Party presidential candidate John Hospers believed that libertarianism is "a philosophy of personal liberty – the liberty of each person to live according to his own choices, provided that he does not attempt to coerce others and thus prevent them from living according to their choices."[4] And American philosopher Robert Nozick claimed that if a moral view goes beyond libertarian side-constraints that only prohibit interference, it cannot avoid the prospect of continually interfering with people's lives.[5]

Taking liberty as the absence of interference by other people from doing what they otherwise either want or are just able to do, libertarians go on to characterize their political ideal as requiring that each person should have the greatest amount of liberty morally commensurate with the greatest amount of liberty for everyone else. Interpreting their ideal in this way, libertarians claim to derive a number of more specific requirements, in particular, a right to life; a right to freedom of speech, press, and assembly; and a right to property.

Here it is important to observe that the libertarian's right to life is not a right to receive from others the goods and resources necessary for preserving one's life; it is simply a right not to have one's life interfered with or ended unjustly. Correspondingly, the libertarian's right to property is not a right to receive from others the goods and resources necessary for one's welfare, but, rather, typically a right not to be interfered with in regard to any goods and resources that one has legitimately acquired either by initial acquisition or by voluntary agreement.

Supporting examples

In support of their view, libertarians have advanced examples of the following sort. The first two are adapted from American economist and Nobel laureate Milton Friedman, the third from Robert Nozick.

In the first example, you are to suppose you and three friends are walking along the street and you happen to notice and retrieve a $100 bill lying on the pavement. Imagine a rich fellow had passed by earlier throwing away $100 bills, and you have been lucky enough to find one of them. According to Friedman, it would be nice of you to share your good fortune with your friends. Nevertheless, they have no right to demand that you do so, and hence they would not be justified in forcing you to share the $100 bill with them. Similarly, Friedman would have us believe that it would be nice of us to provide welfare to the less fortunate members of our society. Nevertheless, the less fortunate members have no right to welfare, and hence they would not be justified in forcing us to provide such.

The second example, which Friedman regards as analogous to the first, involves supposing that there are four Robinson Crusoes, each marooned on four unin-habited islands in the same archipelago. One of these

Crusoes happens to land on a large and fruitful island, which enables him to live easily and well. The others happen to land on tiny and rather barren islands from which they can barely scratch out a living. Suppose one day they discover the existence of each other. Now, according to Friedman, it would be nice of the fortunate Robinson Crusoe to share the resources of his island with the other three Crusoes, but the other three Crusoes have no right to demand that he share those resources, and it would be wrong of them to force him to do so. Correspondingly, Friedman thinks it would be nice of us to provide the less fortunate in our society with welfare, but the less fortunate have no right to demand that we do so, and it would be wrong of them to force us to do so.

In the third example, Robert Nozick asks us to imagine that we are in a society that has just distributed income according to some ideal pattern, possibly a pattern of equality. We are further to imagine that in such a society someone with the athletic talents of LeBron James offers to play basketball for us provided that he receives, let us say, $10 from every home game ticket that is sold. Suppose we agree to these terms, and 2 million people attend the home games to see James play, thereby securing for him an income of $20 million. Since such an income would surely upset the initial pattern of income distribution, whatever that happened to be, Nozick contends that this illustrates how an ideal of liberty upsets the patterns required by other conceptions of justice, and hence calls for their rejection.

Of course, libertarians allow that it would be nice of the rich to share their surplus goods and resources with the poor, just as Milton Friedman would allow that it would be nice of you to share the $100 you found with your friends, and nice of the rich-islanded Robinson Crusoe to share his resources with the poor-islanded Robinson Crusoes. Nevertheless, they deny that government has a duty to provide for such needs. Some good

things, such as providing welfare to the poor, are requirements of charity rather than justice, libertarians claim.
Accordingly, failure to make such provisions is neither
blameworthy nor punishable. As a consequence, such
acts of charity should not be coercively required. For
this reason, libertarians are opposed to tax-supported
welfare programs.

So Kant's ethical theory has given rise to two seemingly divergent perspectives in contemporary ethics: a
welfare liberal perspective that supports the right to
welfare; and a libertarian perspective that rejects any
such right. The welfare liberal perspective appeals to an
ideal of fairness found in Kant's view to support its right
to welfare. The libertarian perspective appeals to an
ideal of liberty also found in Kant's view to reject such
a right. Is it then possible to argue in some nonquestion-
begging way that an ideal of fairness has moral priority
over an ideal of liberty, or vice versa? It is not clear how
one would do this. Alternatively, is there then some
more general moral ideal – such as an ideal of respect –
that can be shown to favor one of these two ideals over
the other? Again, it is not clear how one would show
this. For example, both ideals of fairness and liberty can
be legitimately construed to be interpretations of the
more general ideal of respect, which, therefore, cannot
be used to choose between them.

At this point, some contemporary philosophers, notably Alasdair MacIntyre, have argued that we are facing
incommensurable ideals here with no nonarbitrary way
of choosing between them. Still, there may be a reasonable way of making a choice in this particular case.
Suppose the libertarian ideal of liberty could be shown
to support the same right to welfare that is supported by
the welfare liberal ideal of fairness. Surely, this would
be a welcomed resolution of the conflict between these
two seemingly different interpretations of Kant's and
Aristotle's ethical theories. Yet could libertarians really
be mistaken about what their ideal of liberty requires?

Conflicting liberties

In order to see if this is the case, consider a typical conflict situation between the rich and the poor. In this conflict situation, the rich, of course, have more than enough resources to satisfy their basic needs.[6] In contrast, imagine that the poor lack the resources to meet their basic needs so as to secure a decent life for themselves, even though they have tried all the means available to them that libertarians regard as legitimate for acquiring such resources. Under circumstances like these, libertarians maintain that the rich should have the liberty to use their resources to satisfy their luxury needs if they so wish. Libertarians recognize that this liberty might well be enjoyed with the consequence that the satisfaction of the basic needs of the poor will not be met; they just think that liberty always has priority over other political ideals, and since they assume that the liberty of the poor is not at stake in such conflict situations, it is easy for them to conclude that the rich should not be required to sacrifice their liberty so that the basic needs of the poor may be met.

Of course, libertarians allow that it would be nice of the rich to share their surplus resources with the poor. Nevertheless, according to libertarians, such acts of charity are not required because the liberty of the poor is not thought to be at stake in such conflict situations. In fact, however, the liberty of the poor is at stake in such conflict situations. What is at stake is the liberty of the poor not to be interfered with in taking from the surplus possessions of the rich what is necessary to satisfy their basic needs.

Now when the conflict between the rich and the poor is viewed as a conflict of liberties, either we can say that the rich should have the liberty not to be interfered with in using their surplus resources for luxury purposes, or we can say that the poor should have the liberty not to be interfered with in taking from the rich what they require to meet their basic needs. If we choose one liberty, we must reject the other. What needs to be determined, therefore, is which liberty is morally enforceable: the liberty of the rich or the liberty of the poor.[7]

An expanded "Ought" implies "Can" principle
Now to see why the liberty of the poor, understood as the liberty not to be interfered with when taking from the surplus resources of others what is required to meet one's basic needs, is morally preferable to the liberty of the rich, understood as the liberty not to be interfered with when using one's surplus resources for luxury purposes, we need only appeal again, as we did earlier, to an expanded "Ought" implies "Can" principle, a principle that combines the traditional "Ought" implies "Can" principle with the widespread conviction that morality cannot impose unreasonable requirements on anyone. According to this principle, people are not morally required to do either what they lack the power to do or what would involve so great a sacrifice or restriction that it would be unreasonable to require them to perform such an action.

Now, applying this expanded "Ought" implies "Can" principle to the case at hand, it seems clear that the poor have it within their power to relinquish such an important liberty as the liberty not to be interfered with when taking from the rich what they require to meet their basic needs. They could do this. Nevertheless, it is unreasonable in this context to require them to accept so great a restriction. In the extreme case, it involves requiring the poor to sit back and starve to death. Of course, the poor may have no real alternative to relinquishing this liberty. To do anything else may involve worse consequences for themselves and their loved ones and may invite a painful death. Accordingly, we may expect that the poor would accede, albeit unwillingly, to a political system that denied them the right to welfare supported by such a liberty, at the same time we recognize that such a system has imposed an unreasonable restriction upon the poor – a restriction that we could not morally blame them for trying to evade. Analogously, we might expect that a woman whose life is threatened would submit to a rapist's demands, at the same time that we recognize the utter unreasonableness of those demands.

By contrast, it is not unreasonable to require the rich in this context to sacrifice the liberty to meet some of their luxury needs so that the poor can have the liberty to meet their basic needs. Naturally, we might expect that the rich, for reasons of self-interest or past contribution, might be disinclined to make such a sacrifice. We might even suppose that the past contributions of the rich provide a good reason for not sacrificing their liberty to use their surplus for luxury purposes. Yet the rich cannot claim that relinquishing such a liberty involves so great a sacrifice that it is unreasonable to require them to make it. So it is the rich here, and not the poor, who are morally blameworthy and subject to coercion for failing to make the appropriate sacrifice.

Consequently, if we assume that however else we specify the requirements of morality, they cannot violate an expanded "Ought" implies "Can" principle, it follows that, despite what libertarians claim, the right to liberty endorsed by them actually favors the liberty of the poor over the liberty of the rich.

Libertarian objections

Yet couldn't libertarians object to this conclusion, claiming that it would be unreasonable to require the rich to sacrifice the liberty to meet some of their luxury needs so that the poor can have the liberty to meet their basic needs? As I have pointed out, libertarians don't usually see the situation as a conflict of liberties, but suppose they did. How plausible would such an objection be?

Consider: What are libertarians going to say about the poor? Isn't it clearly unreasonable to require the poor to restrict their liberty to meet their basic needs so that the rich can have the liberty to meet their luxury needs? Isn't it clearly unreasonable to coercively require the poor to sit back and starve to death? If so, no resolution of this conflict is reasonable to coercively require both the rich and the poor to accept. But that would mean that libertarians could not be putting forth a moral resolution, because a moral resolution, according to an expanded "Ought" implies "Can" principle, resolves severe conflicts of interest in ways reasonable to require everyone affected to accept, where it is further understood that a moral resolution can sometimes require us to act in accord with altruistic reasons. Therefore, as long as libertarians think of themselves as putting forth a moral resolution, they cannot allow that it is unreasonable in cases of severe conflict of interest both to require the rich to restrict their liberty to meet their luxury needs in order to benefit the poor and to require the poor to restrict their liberty to meet their basic needs in order to benefit the rich. But if one of these requirements is to be judged reasonable, then, by any neutral assessment, it must be the requirement that the rich restrict their liberty to meet their luxury needs so that the poor can have the liberty to meet their basic needs. There is no other plausible resolution, if libertarians intend to put forth a moral resolution.

Now it might also be objected that the right to welfare that this argument establishes from libertarian premises is not the same as the right to welfare endorsed by welfare liberals and socialists. This is correct. We could mark this difference by referring to the right that this argument establishes as "a negative welfare right" and by referring to the right endorsed by welfare liberals as "a positive welfare right." The significance of this difference is that a person's negative welfare right can be violated only when other people, through acts of commission, interfere with its exercise, whereas a person's positive welfare right can be violated not only by such acts of commission but by acts of omission as well. For example, just letting the poor starve to death (an act of omission but not one of commission) would not violate the poor's negative right to welfare but it would violate their positive right to welfare if they had one.

Nonetheless, this difference will have little practical import because in recognizing the legitimacy of negative welfare rights, libertarians will come to see that virtually any use of their surplus possessions is likely to violate the negative welfare rights of the poor by preventing the poor from rightfully appropriating (some part of) their surplus goods and resources. So, in order to ensure that they will not be engaging in such wrongful actions, it will be incumbent on them to set up institutions guaranteeing adequate positive welfare rights for the poor. Only then will they be able to use legitimately any remaining surplus possessions to meet their own nonbasic needs. Furthermore, in the absence of adequate positive welfare rights, the poor, acting either by themselves or through their allies or agents, would have some discretion in determining when and how to exercise their negative welfare rights. In order not to be subject to that discretion, libertarians will tend to favor the only morally legitimate way of preventing the exercise of such rights: They will set up institutions guaranteeing adequate positive welfare rights that will then take precedence over the exercise of negative welfare rights. For these reasons, recognizing the negative welfare rights of the poor will ultimately lead libertarians to endorse the same sort of welfare institutions favored by welfare liberals.

Rand's No-Duty thesis

As we have seen, what Rand is most committed to denying is that we have a duty to help the poor when we are rich or talented. Yet if there is no duty to help in such situations, then the rich and talented would be within their rights to refuse to help, and the poor would have no moral recourse in the face of such a refusal. At the extreme, this would mean that the poor would be required to sit back and starve to death while the rich and talented were allowed to enjoy the benefit of their luxuries. Yet surely this would be an unreasonable requirement to impose on the poor, one that would violate what I have called the expanded "Ought" implies "Can" principle. According to this principle, morality cannot impose unreasonable demands on people. In the extreme case, requiring the poor to sit back and starve to death would clearly be an unreasonable demand, whereas requiring the rich and talented to forgo meeting some of their luxury needs would clearly not be an unreasonable demand.

Alternatively, we could use the expanded "Ought" implies "Can" principle to weigh the liberty of the poor against the liberty of the rich, as we did in our discussion of the libertarian interpretation of Kantian ethics. Either way, the principle would support a duty to help the poor when their basic needs would not otherwise be met, or, as Rand puts it, when their survival as rational human beings through their whole lifespan is threatened.[8]

Rand, therefore, fails to establish that the only fundamental virtue that Aristotelian ethics needs is that of selfishness. As we have shown, Aristotelian ethics also needs a virtue of altruism that is sufficient to support a duty to help the poor when they are in need. Not surprisingly, the altruism required here will resemble the moderate form of altruism that is supported by a welfare liberal interpretation of Kantian and consequentialist ethics.[9]

Appealing to the principle of nonquestion-beggingness
Let us now see how we can get to the same conclusion that we just derived by appealing to the expanded "Ought" implies "Can" principle by appealing to the even more fundamental normative principle of nonquestion-beggingness – a requirement for a good argument

that we used in Chapter 2. Here, we will be applying it to conflicting liberties instead of to the conflicting interests to which we applied it when we were using the principle to provide a justification of morality.

As before, we will need to idealize a bit. First, consider a ranking of your liberties from your most important to your least important. Then consider a ranking of liberties of others from their most important liberties to their least important liberties.

Now some of the liberties in these rankings will not be in conflict, so you exercising your liberties will be fully compatible with other people exercising their liberties. Clearly, for such cases, both your liberties and the liberties of others should be promoted.

Nevertheless, there will also be other situations where your liberties come into conflict with the liberties of others. Let us set aside those cases where your high-ranking liberties come into conflict with the high-ranking liberties of others – these cases are like lifeboat cases and any view is going to have some difficulty resolving them. Far more numerous are cases where your high-ranking liberties come into conflict with the low-ranking liberties of others or their high-ranking liberties come into conflict with your low-ranking liberties. Let us now focus on just such conflict cases between the rich and the poor.

Here we are also given that we are dealing with a situation where we must have an enforceable resolution one way or the other. Given the importance of the liberties that are at stake, what is to be done here cannot be left up to arbitrary choice or sheer power.

So here we need to appeal to the priorities that are determined by the principle of nonquestion-beggingness and have high-ranking liberties enforceably trump low-ranking liberties in these conflict situations. In this way, the high-ranking liberties of the poor in having their basic needs met will enforceably trump the low-ranking liberties of the rich in being able to use their surplus for luxury purposes, and this, I claim, will ground a right to welfare.

In brief, then, I have argued that a libertarian ideal of liberty can be seen to support a right to welfare by applying both an expanded "Ought" implies "Can" principle and the even more fundamental principle of nonquestion-beggingness to conflicts between the rich and the poor. These principles support such rights by favoring the liberty of the poor over the liberty of the rich. Clearly, what is crucial to the derivation of these rights is that according to the expanded "Ought" implies "Can" principle, it would be unreasonable to require the poor to deny their basic needs and accept anything less than these rights as the condition for their willing cooperation, and according to the principle of nonquestion-beggingness, only that result has the support of a good argument. These arguments should be more than sufficient to achieve the second reconciliation we sought between consequentialism and nonconsequentialism.

The third reconciliation

Our third task of reconciliation was to reconcile consequentialism, in general, with Kantian and Aristotelian ethics. Clearly, this task is much easier to accomplish now that we have achieved the first two reconciliations. We now recognize that both consequentialists and nonconsequentialists are committed to using the expanded "Ought" implies "Can" principle to limit the exceptions to the Pauline principle, and that they are also committed to using that same expanded "Ought" implies "Can" principle together with the principle of nonquestion-beggingness to derive welfare liberal conclusions from libertarian premises. Accordingly, providing a general reconciliation of consequentialism with Kantian and Aristotelian ethics should be much easier to achieve.

What needs to be recognized is that each ethical view brings a different emphasis to the reconciliation. Thus, consequentialism brings an emphasis on consequences, while Kantian ethics brings an emphasis on universalizability which implies that what is right for one person to do is also right for others who are in relevantly similar circumstances.

But what about Aristotelian ethics? What emphasis does it bring to the reconciliation? Here the answer has to be its emphasis on virtue, but notice that this makes the Aristotelian contribution to the reconciliation of a different order from that of the other views. The emphasis of consequentialism on consequences and the emphasis of Kantian ethics on universalizability have a first-order character to them. This is because they provide a nonmoral standard of what is morally right. The Aristotelian emphasis on virtue, however, is different; it is not a first-order standard for determining what is morally right because it does not provide any nonmoral standard for doing so.[10]

Fortunately, that does not create a problem for reconciling these three theories of ethics. We only need to recognize the different contributions they each make to their reconciliation. Moreover, consequentialists, Kantians, and Aristotelians today are all committed to taking all relevant interests fairly into account, and that commitment, along with their commitment to the expanded "Ought" implies "Can" principle, should secure equal status for the theories while reconciling them in practice. It is in this way, therefore, that the third reconciliation of consequentialist with nonconsequentialist ethics can be achieved.

Conclusion

In sum, in this chapter we have been able to:

1 reconcile consequentialism with the Pauline principle requirement never to do evil that good may come of it, which is endorsed by nonconsequentialists, by using the expanded "Ought" implies "Can" principle;
2 reconcile libertarian interpretations of Kant's and Aristotle's ethics with alternative welfare liberal interpretations of those views by arguing from libertarian premises and using the expanded "Ought" implies "Can" principle and the even more widely endorsed principle of nonquestion-beggingness; and
3 reconcile consequentialism, in general, with Kantian and Aristotelian ethics by recognizing their commitment to the expanded "Ought" implies "Can" principle, as well as the different contributions they bring to that reconciliation.

6

Morality and Religion

The *Euthyphro* question

In Plato's *Euthyphro*, Socrates raises a fundamental question about morality. We can state the question as follows:

- Are actions right because God commands them, or
- Does God command actions because they are right?

According to the first option, morality is fundamentally dependent on religion. According to the second, morality is fundamentally independent of religion in such a way that even God, if he exists, would have to affirm. In this dialogue, Socrates slowly maneuvers Euthyphro into endorsing the second option, affirming that God commands actions because they are right, and, hence, that morality is fundamentally independent of religion. This is an alternative that is still favored by many religious believers, and usually, but not always, by atheists and agnostics as well.[1] However, the first option – that actions are right because God commands them, and, hence, that morality is fundamentally dependent on religion – also has its defenders. These defenders have been appropriately called "divine command theorists" because they identify morality simply with the commands of God.

To illustrate their view, divine command theorists often cite the following story from the Bible. In the book of Genesis, God tells Abraham, "Take your only son Isaac whom you love and go into the district of Mona and there offer him as a holocaust on a hill which I shall point out to you." Abraham does as he is told, but as he is about to sacrifice his son, an angel of the Lord stops him by telling him, "I know now that you fear God, since you have not withheld your only son." And later he is told, "Since you have done this, and have not withheld your only son, I will indeed bless you and will surely multiply your descendants as the stars of the heavens and sands of the seashore."[2]

In this story, Abraham does not argue with God, as he had done on an earlier occasion when God proposed to destroy Sodom and Gomorrah. At that time, Abraham argued with God and got a reprieve for the cities if "fifty just men" could be found in them. He then went on to get the requirement of fifty reduced to just ten. In this way, Abraham exhibited a willingness to argue with God.

With respect to God's command to sacrifice his own son, however, Abraham does not argue with him at all. Rather, he immediately takes steps to do just what God commands him to do. In the end, Abraham is not required by God to make the ultimate sacrifice of his son. Instead, God is satisfied with Abraham's willingness to do what he was commanded to do, and for that Abraham is said to have been rewarded handsomely.

Now the biblical story of Abraham's near-sacrifice of his son has been taken to illustrate divine command theory. It purports to show how an action that we might otherwise think is wrong – intentionally killing one's own innocent child – could be made the right thing to do simply by the commands of God.

Medieval developments of divine command theory

During the Middle Ages, William of Ockham (1280–1349) extends this same divine command theory analysis to other actions: "The hatred of God, theft, adultery, and actions similar to these actions . . . can be performed meritoriously by an earthly pilgrim if they should come under divine precepts."[3] In support of the same view, another medieval philosopher, Thomas Aquinas (1225–74), provides the following explanation:

> Adultery is intercourse with another's wife, who is allotted to him by the law emanating from God. Consequently, intercourse with any woman by the command of God is neither adultery nor fornication. The same applies to theft, which is the taking of another's property. For whatever is taken by the command of God, to whom all things belong, is not taken against the will of its owner, whereas it is in that that theft consists.[4]

So what Ockham and Aquinas are saying here is that acts which previously were wrong, such as intentionally killing an innocent person, theft, adultery, even hatred of God, are transformed into acts that should be done if and when God commands them to be performed. This is because what made them wrong in the first place was simply that God commanded that they not be done. So if God were now to command differently with respect to those actions – command that they be done rather than that they not be done – then the moral character of them would change from being morally prohibited to being morally required.

Problems for divine command theory

However, there are two significant problems for divine command theory that need to be addressed:

1 How are we to understand God's commands?
2 How are we to identify God's commands?

Let us examine each of these problems in turn.

How are we to understand God's commands?

Suppose we had a list of God's commands, how should we understand them? We might think of God as a one-person legislature with ourselves having a role similar to the judiciary and executive branches of government. God, as the one-person legislature, would make the commands/laws, and we, as the judiciary/executive, would have the task of interpreting and applying those commands/laws.

Of course, there would be differences. The U.S. judiciary, in interpreting the laws, often tries to determine what purpose the legislature had in passing particular laws, and whether that purpose accords with the U.S. Constitution. And sometimes the U.S. judiciary strikes down laws passed by the legislature as not in accord with the U.S. Constitution.

According to divine command theory, however, there wouldn't be any comparable role for humans to have with respect to the commands of God. We couldn't, for example, strike down any of God's commands because they failed to accord with some independent standard. Thus, our role in interpreting and applying God's commands would be narrowly circumscribed.

Even so, there are further problems understanding what that role would be.

This is because divine commands presumably could come into conflict. Thus, suppose we had one divine command that we should each love and care for the members of our family and another that we should love and care for the deserving poor wherever they are. Surely, these two commands would conflict when we are faced with the option of using our limited resources either to provide luxuries for the members of our family or to use those same resources to provide for the basic needs of the deserving poor elsewhere. Here we seem to require some kind of a background theory that compares what good would be accomplished in each case, as well as weighs the competing obligations involved, and then makes a recommendation about what should be done.

Yet divine command theory does not provide any such background theory for resolving conflicts between commands. According to the theory, each command is obligatory simply because it is commanded by God. Conflicts that arise among God's commands could be appropriately resolved only by another command of God that indicates which command is to have priority. This is because, according to divine command theory, the resolution always could go either way. So there is no way for us to figure out, in advance, how it should go. This, then, would leave us with a very minimal role when interpreting or applying the commands of God, and in cases where those commands conflict, we would be at a complete loss as to what to do.

How are we to identify God's commands?

Another problem with divine command theory is how to determine what God has actually commanded us to do. It would seem that divine command theorists maintain that God's commands are communicated through special revelations to particular individuals or groups. But if the commands of God are made known only to a select few, how are others to know what those commands are or when they are reasonably bound to obey them? Presumably, people can be morally bound to obey only by commands they know about and have reason to accept.

To add an additional complication, different individuals and groups have claimed to be recipients of different special revelations that conflict in ways which would support conflicting moral requirements. Of course, if some of those who claim to have received a special revelation rise to power, they may be able to force obedience on the rest. But if that happens, others may have no independent reason to go along with that forceful imposition.

Radically modified divine command theory

To deal with these problems of divine command theory, some philosophers have distinguished between general and special revelations as sources of God's commands. According to Stephen Evans, "[General] revelation is the knowledge of God that God makes possible through observation of the natural world and through reflections on human experiences that are universal and commonly accessible."[5] This is, of course, to recognize creation as a relatively independent source of moral requirements. Most importantly, it has the effect of radically modifying divine command theory. As the theory was originally formulated, moral requirements were determined simply by the commands of God. God could make anything right or wrong simply by commanding differently without making any change in our human nature or the circumstances of our lives.

Yet faced with conflicting special revelations, what else were divine command theorists to do? There was a clear need to appeal to a common ground to deal with apparently conflicting requirements of different special revelations. So that common ground was taken to be provided by normative requirements (i.e., the dos and don'ts) that are grounded in our nature and circumstances. Of course, it is also open for divine command theorists to claim that their own favored special revelation provides the best interpretation of the normative requirements that are grounded in our nature and our circumstances. At the same time, atheists and agnostics could also accept those normative requirements that are grounded in our nature and circumstances as their sole basis for moral requirements. For the religious person, however, there remain two sources of morality:

- one being the normative requirements that are grounded in our nature and circumstances, or, put another way, what can be known about the requirements of morality through reason alone;
- the other being what can be known about the requirements of morality through special revelation.

Hence, there still is the problem of what should be done if and when these two purported sources of morality come into conflict, especially in the public arena.

Religion and the public arena

Attempting to deal with just this problem, John Rawls has argued that in the public arena, citizens should conduct their fundamental discussions within the framework of public reason, appealing only to reasons that others "can reasonably be expected to endorse."[6] Since not all citizens in liberal, pluralistic societies can reasonably be expected to share the same religious perspective, Rawls proposed that reliance on public reason rule out any role for religious considerations in public debate over fundamental issues in such societies. This is because legislation must be sufficiently supported by reasons that are accessible to everyone to whom that legislation applies, and religious reasons are usually not claimed to have this general accessibility.

Now it might be objected that the relevant religious reasons are accessible to virtually everyone and so this would serve to suffice to justify legislation that is based on them. For example, to assert that Christian moral teachings as such are accessible to everyone is to say that these teachings are accessible as part of a unique Christian salvation history, which has, as key events, an Incarnation, a Redemptive Death, and a Resurrection. But let's examine this claim.

Surely, some religious moral teachings can be given a justification that is independent of the religion in which they are found (e.g., the parable of the Good Samaritan[7]) – a justification that is accessible to virtually everyone on the grounds that virtually everyone would be able to understand that it would be unreasonable to reject those religious moral teachings so justified.[8] But the claim we are considering is not about justifying religious teachings in this way. Rather, it claims that religious moral teachings are justified as part of a distinctive religious tradition, with the consequence that it would be unreasonable for virtually anyone to reject them on that account.

But is this the case? Surely, for example, many Christian moral teachings are understandable to both Christians and non-Christians alike, but the sense of "accessible" we have been using implies more than this. It implies that persons can be morally blamed for failing to abide by such requirements because they can come to understand that these requirements apply to them as part of a unique Christian salvation history, which has, as key events, an Incarnation, a Redemptive Death, and a Resurrection, and that it would be unreasonable for them to fail to abide by them on that account. So understood, it would seem that Christian moral teachings as such are not accessible to everyone. Too many non-Christians, who seem otherwise moral, do not recognize the authority of Christian moral teachings as such, even though they may grant that some of these teachings have an independent justification. And the same would hold true here for non-Christian religious moral teachings as well.

Accordingly, religious moral teachings as such cannot serve as a substitute for accessible substantive reasons, like a set of constraints modeled somewhat after those found in the U.S. Constitution or the European Convention of Human Rights, which are needed, along with democratic procedural reasons, to morally justify legislation that everyone should abide by. If legislation is to be morally justified, there must always be accessible procedural and substantive reasons, which, taken together, constitute a sufficient justification to coercively require everyone to abide by that legislation. Accordingly, our ethical norms require us to provide sufficient nonreligious justifications for whatever coercive measures we want to impose on others.

Ethical norms and the problem of evil

Yet it is also important to realize that our ethical norms have an even more significant role to play with respect to religion. This is because it has long been argued that our ethical norms are incompatible with the existence of an all-good, all-powerful God. An early formulation of this argument, purportedly attributed to Epicurus (341–270 BCE), went as follows:

> Is God willing to prevent evil, but not able? Then he is not omnipotent.
> Is he able, but not willing? Then he is malevolent.
> Is he both able and willing? Then whence cometh evil?
> Is he neither able nor willing? Then why call him God?

Over the centuries, this argument, expressed in one way or another, has given rise to what has been called the problem of evil. This is the problem of whether, in light of our ethical norms, an all-good, all-powerful God is compatible with the evil that exists in the world.

Now in the classical world, the problem of evil might have at least sometimes been taken as a challenge to the very existence of God or gods. The historical evidence here is a bit mixed. For example, even Epicurus, the purported author of the above argument, allowed that gods might exist, although they had nothing to do with human affairs.

During the Middle Ages, however, the problem of evil was definitely taken to be limited to the challenge of providing some explanation for why an all-good, all-powerful God would permit the evil that we find in the world. Virtually no one during the Middle Ages thought that the evil in the world was incompatible with the very existence of the God of traditional theism. Yet with the coming of the European Enlightenment, and especially in the writing of David Hume and Baron d'Holbach, just such an interpretation of the problem of evil began to emerge.

Later in the 19th century, Charles Darwin was deeply troubled by the problem of evil, particularly with regard to the natural evil in the world. Just a few months after publishing his *The Origin of Species*, Darwin wrote to Harvard botanist Asa Gray, a staunch believer:

> I had no intention to write atheistically. But I own that I cannot see as plainly as others do, and as I should wish to do, evidence of design and beneficence on all sides of us. There seems to be too much misery in the world. I cannot persuade myself that a beneficent and omnipotent God would have designedly created the Ichneumonidae [a species of caterpillar] with the express intention of their [larvae] feeding within the living bodies of caterpillars.[9]

Darwin clearly thought that his theory of evolution made it even more difficult to show that an all-good, all-powerful God was compatible with all the evil in the world.

In the 20th century, John Mackie restated the problem of evil in its more challenging form as follows:

> God is omnipotent; God is wholly good; and yet evil exists. There seems to be some contradiction between these three propositions, so that if any two of them were true the third would be false. But at the same time all three are essential parts of most theological positions: the theologian, it seems, at once must and cannot consistently adhere to all three.[10]

Yet today the tide has seemingly changed because it is widely held by theists and atheists alike that Alvin Plantinga essentially solved the problem of evil as formulated by Mackie.[11] What Plantinga was thought to have shown is that it may not be within God's power to bring about a world containing moral good but no moral evil, and so the existence of at least some evil in the world raises no problem at all for the existence of the God of traditional theism.[12] Plantinga argued that this is because to bring about a world containing moral good, God would have to permit persons to act freely, and it may well be that in every possible world where God actually permits persons to act freely, everyone would suffer from a malady that Plantinga labeled "Transworld Depravity," which meant that everyone would act wrongly at least to some degree. Accepting Plantinga's defense, both theists and atheists have been willing to grant that it may be logically impossible for God to create a world with moral agents like ourselves that does not also have at least some moral evil in it. Thus, it is generally agreed by theists and atheists alike that a good God is logically compatible with some moral evil, and the only question they now want to pursue is how probable or improbable it is that God is compatible with all the evil that exists in the world.

Nevertheless, there is a better way to approach the problem of evil posed by Mackie. The general approach favored by Plantinga and others has been to come up with possible, even plausible, constraints on God's power that would serve to account for evil in the world. Yet what about seeing evil in the world as required by God's goodness rather than simply being required by constraints on God's power?[13] Surely, we have no difficulty seeing at least some of the natural evil in the world in this light. Think, for example, of the pain most of us experience when we get too close to fire. Clearly, a good God would want us to experience pain in such contexts. Now consider a doctor who pushes and shoves her way through a crowded subway in order to come to the aid of someone who is having a heart attack. Or consider your not being fully honest with a temporarily depressed friend to keep him from doing something he would deeply regret later.[14] Arguably, a good God would have no difficulty permitting (hence, not interfering with) such minor moral wrongs, given the greater evil that would thereby be prevented. That admission appears to be all that is needed to solve the problem of evil posed by Mackie, but it is a solution based on an appeal to God's goodness rather than simply to any constraint on God's power.[15] So the idea is to appeal to God's goodness to explain why his power has not been exercised in a certain regard rather than appeal to (a limitation of) God's power to explain why he has not done some particular good.

Notice that underlying this alternative approach to solving the problem of evil posed by Mackie is a commitment to the following moral principle.

Noninterference

Every moral agent has reason not to interfere with the free actions of wrongdoers when permitting the slightly harmful consequences of those actions would lead to securing some significant moral good, in some cases maybe just that of the freedom of the wrongdoers themselves, or to preventing some significant moral evil.

Clearly, noninterference holds of ourselves, but it also holds of God, and, on that account, it seems to permit a solution to the problem of evil posed by Mackie. And this seems right. The morality that is operative here is appropriately a morality that applies to all moral agents, ourselves as well as God.

Yet what we now need to do is turn to the task of determining what moral principle or principles holding of God and ourselves apply to the degree and amount of moral evil in the world. This new task need not be seen as moving from a logical problem of evil to something else – an evidential problem of evil where the existence of God is no longer an issue of logical possibility or logical impossibility but rather one of probability or improbability. Rather, in seeking to determine the compatibility of God and the degree and amount of moral evil in our world, there is no reason to think that we are dealing with a really different kind of problem of evil from the one posed by Mackie. This looks like just another logical problem of evil where the question at issue is whether there is some other moral principle that holds of ourselves, and should hold of God as well, which is consistent or inconsistent with the existence of God.

Now from our discussion of both consequential and nonconsequential theories of ethics, one such principle that immediately comes to the fore is the Pauline principle that we should never do evil that good may come of it.

Of course, the Pauline principle has been rejected as an absolute principle. This is because, as we noted in the previous chapter, there clearly seem to be exceptions to it when the resulting evil or harm is:

1 trivial (e.g., as in the case of stepping on someone's foot to get out of a crowded subway);
2 easily reparable (e.g., as in the case of lying to a temporarily depressed friend to keep him from committing suicide); and, more significantly,
3 the only way to prevent a far greater harm to innocent people (e.g., as in the case of shooting one of twenty civilian hostages to prevent, in the only way possible, the execution of all twenty).

Yet despite the belief that there are exceptions to the principle, and despite the disagreement over the extent of those exceptions, the Pauline principle still plays an important role in ethical theory, as we have seen in Chapter 4.

Given, then, that there are standard exceptions to the Pauline principle, might not God's permission of evil fall under them? Well, consider how morally constrained these standard exceptions to the Pauline principle are. They allow us to do evil that good may come of it only when the evil is trivial, easily reparable, or the only way to prevent a far greater harm to innocents. So it is difficult to see how God's widespread permission of the harmful consequences of significantly evil actions, which is not of these sorts, could be a justified exception to the Pauline principle.

In addition, the standard exceptions that are allowed only seem to be allowed because the agents involved lack the power to accomplish the good or avoid the evil in any other way. Yet clearly God is not subject to any such limitation of power. Thus, God can negotiate crowded subways without harming anyone in the slightest. God can also prevent a temporarily depressed person from committing suicide without lying to them, and God can save all twenty civilian hostages without having to execute any one of them. Consequently, none of these exceptions to the Pauline principle that are permitted to agents like ourselves, because of our limited power, would hold for God. So God, if he exists, would not be subject to any causal constraints with respect to preventing evils. Nor would it make sense to say that where we are just subject to causal constraints, God is subject to logical constraints, because that would make God impossibly less powerful than we are.

Now it might be objected here that while God cannot do evil that good may come of it, God could permit evil that good may come of it. Of course, moral philosophers do recognize a distinction between doing and permitting evil. Doing evil is normally worse than permitting evil. But when the evil is significant and one can easily prevent it, then permitting evil can become morally equivalent to doing it. The same kind of moral blame attaches to both actions. Think of someone who permitted a family member to be brutally raped. Surely the "permitting" here has the same moral status as a "doing." Likewise, God's permitting significantly evil consequences when those consequences can easily be prevented is morally equivalent to God's doing something that is seriously wrong.

It might also be objected that God is not really intending evil consequences at all but merely foreseeing their occurrence, or, put another way, God is intentionally doing something, that is, making us free, but then he is only foreseeing the evil consequences that result therefrom. Yet God is said to be permitting those evil consequences, and permitting is an intentional act. So if God intends not to stop the evil consequences of our actions when he can easily do so, then he is not merely foreseeing those consequences.

So, given that God is not subject to any causal constraint with respect to the prevention of horrendous evil consequences of immoral actions, and given that permitting evil can be as bad as doing it and that God's permitting evil could not be just a foreseeing of it, the question remains: Could, in light of our ethical norms, an all-good, all-powerful God be compatible with all the evil that exists in the world? Surely this is an ethical question as important as any we face in our lives.[16]

Conclusion

We started off this chapter with the central question that Socrates raises in Plato's *Euthyphro*: Are actions right because God commands them, or does God command actions because they are right? We then pursued the answer given by divine command theorists that actions are right simply because God commands them. We saw how divine command theorists did not want to rely on the normative structure of human nature and the circumstances of our lives as a source of morality, but that they were forced to do so because of the various problems facing their theory. We then considered what to do when the requirements of the normative structure of our nature and circumstances come into conflict with the requirements of special revelations in the public arena. Here we saw that fairness required that there be sufficient reasons accessible to the minority to justify coercively requiring it to accept the will of the majority. Finally, we considered whether the norms of morality might actually be in conflict with the very existence of an all-good, all-powerful God owing to the severity and amount of evil in the world.

7

Conclusion

This book promised that it would help you make the ethical choices that you confront in your lives. Now it is time for you to determine how successful the book has been in that endeavor. Consider what this book has done for you.

Two challenges

The book began with a general account of ethics. It then took up the challenge of ethical relativism. That challenge was given its day in court and found wanting. Here the normative requirements of human nature and the circumstances of our lives were seen to provide an independent source of morality.

Egoism was also seen to provide a significant challenge to ethics. Egoism challenged the very existence of moral requirements. It claimed that we should just serve our own self-interest. But it, too, was found wanting. Morality was shown to be rationally preferable to egoism.

Two conceptions

That still left the problem of how best to interpret ethics. Traditionally, ethics has been given consequentialist and nonconsequentialist interpretations. We then evaluated each of these interpretations.

Consequentialist ethics requires us to always choose whatever action or social policy would have the best consequences for everyone concerned. We tested this view out to see whether it would recommend the torture favored by former U.S. vice president Cheney and supported by the British government, or the terrorism favored by Osama bin Laden. We discovered that rarely, if ever, would such actions be justified, given that there would almost always be other ways to achieve the desired results without using such objectionable means.

Nonconsequentialist ethics was seen to differ from consequentialist ethics by imposing constraints on the pursuit of overall good consequences. Kantian ethics and Aristotelian ethics are its main forms.

Kantian ethics requires us to test our behavior by asking, in effect, what if everyone did that, and then rejecting those actions that cannot be so universalized. By applying this Kantian test to different possible rules for keeping promises, we saw the need to build into the test morally appropriate exceptions to otherwise approved rules.

Aristotelian ethics specifies moral requirements in terms of the virtuous life that is further determined by what a person at a particular stage of development should do next in order to become more virtuous. Ayn Rand's interpretation of Aristotelian ethics required us to reject altruism and make a virtue of selfishness. We found that Rand's account of altruism was overdrawn and that her view is best understood as opposed to a more moderate form of altruism that is actually favored by her opponents.

Reconciliation

We then attempted to reconcile consequentialist and nonconsequentialist ethics in their Kantian and Aristotelian varieties by showing that an expanded "Ought" implies "Can" principle as well as the principle of nonquestion-beggingness internally constrain what each of these views can require. We further showed that consequentialist and nonconsequentialist ethics can be further reconciled once we recognize that both views are committed to taking all relevant interests fairly into account.

Ethics and religion

We then considered whether the norms of morality could be based simply on the commands of God. Here again, as with the challenge of ethical relativism, we recognized that the normative requirements of human nature and the circumstances of our lives provide us with an independent source of morality. At the same time, we recognized that the norms of morality might actually be in conflict with the very existence of an all-good, all-powerful God owing to the severity and the amount of evil in the world.

In this way, traditional ethics, whether consequentialist or nonconsequentialist, when suitably interpreted, can be shown to meet the challenges of ethical relativism, egoism, and religion, and thus maintain its usefulness for helping us make the ethical choices we face in our lives.

Practicing ethics

But how does it do this? Consider a range of moral issues concerning which you will most surely be required to take a stand:

1 the distribution of income and wealth;
2 torture;
3 gay and lesbian concerns;
4 affirmative action;
5 pornography;
6 sexual harassment; and
7 punishment.

Now with respect to each of these issues, let us see how the resources of this book can help you in resolving them.

Issue 1

Approaching the issue of distribution of income and wealth with our reconciliation of consequentialist and nonconsequentialist ethics, we would need to especially take into account the conflicting perspectives of the rich and the poor in our society, and we would need more data about the rich and the poor and the availability of economic resources in our society before we could come up with a morally defensible resolution of this issue.

Still, we could draw an analogy to physics, where the behavior of bodies under certain idealized conditions is considered first, and then only later are other factors such as friction and resistance taken into account. Analogously, we could imagine that the rich have gotten all their wealth legitimately and thus not in any way by coercing or defrauding the poor. Similarly, we could imagine that the poor have unsuccessfully tried all means morally available to them to satisfy their own basic needs. Now if we were to imagine the rich and poor, so characterized, behind a Rawlsian veil of ignorance as discussed in Chapter 5, not knowing whether they are rich or poor, they would surely favor a right to welfare.

Yet if we considered the rich and the poor, so characterized, from a libertarian perspective, the rich could have the liberty not to be interfered with in using their surplus resources for luxury purposes. But then couldn't the poor also be thought to have the liberty not to be interfered with in taking from the surplus of the rich what the poor require in order to meet their basic needs? That would give us a conflict of negative liberties, and then resolving that conflict by using the "Ought" implies "Can" principle or the principle of nonquestion-beggingness, as employed in Chapters 5 and 6, would surely give us a right to welfare.

Moreover, since the libertarian view, in particular, regards rights that are grounded in liberty to be universal rights, this implies that a right to welfare extends to all needy people whether they exist now or only in the future. This would hold insofar as our consumption of resources for luxury purposes leads to needy people being deprived of resources they would require to meet their own basic needs whether just now or only in the future.[1]

So what does this imply? Could it be that those presently existing should use no more resources than they require for a decent life so that needy people around the world today and into the future would also have a decent life? Surely that question deserves further consideration.

Issue 2

With regard to the moral issues of torture, the discussion in Chapter 3 is probably the most relevant. Again, more information and argument would be required to properly resolve these issues. Nevertheless, it seems fairly clear that rarely, if ever, would acts of torture or terror be morally justified given that there would almost always be other ways to achieve the desired results without using such objectionable means. In addition, such means would surely tend to fail to satisfy an expanded "Ought" implies "Can" principle and the principle of nonquestion-beggingness that internally constrains both consequentialist and nonconsequentialist ethics.

Nevertheless, there may be exceptions. For example, advocates for the possible use of torture frequently bring up a hypothetical ticking time-bomb case. We are to imagine that the authorities have in custody a person who knows the location of a deadly bomb hidden in a major European city that is set to explode in twenty-four hours. Is it then morally permissible to torture the person to learn where the bomb is hidden? Some have argued that the use of torture in such a case is objectionable because it would generalize to less extreme cases, and eventually lead to the widespread use of torture. Others have argued that humane ways of interrogating require time to establish a relationship with the person being interrogated, and so would not be effective in the short time available in the ticking time-bomb case. So what should be done?

What about asking: Why has the bomb been planted in the first place? Now it is unlikely that this is part of a military offensive to conquer the country in question. More likely, there is some great wrong or perceived wrong to which the would-be bomber is responding. So what if the authorities were to take steps to remedy, either in whole or in part, the wrong or perceived wrong at issue?[2] Might not the person then reveal where the bomb has been planted? In any case, isn't this just the approach that should be taken to the ticking time-bomb case if all relevant interests are to be taken fairly into account?

Issue 3

Obviously, the issue of gay and lesbian concerns requires its own particular discussion where the relevant facts about gay marriage and homosexual and heterosexual lifestyles and households are brought to bear on the issues. There is, however, one very important contribution that this book does make to such a discussion. It is that the resolution of this issue, involving enforcement as it does, must be justified with sufficient reasons that are accessible to all those to whom it applies. This is because, as was argued in Chapter 6, people cannot be justifiably forced to abide by ethical requirements if they cannot come to know, and so come to justifiably believe, that they should abide by those requirements. For an ethics to justifiably enforce its requirements, there must be sufficient reasons accessible to all those to whom it applies to abide by those requirements. What this means is that the ethics must be secular rather than religious in character because only secular reasons are accessible to everyone; religious reasons are primarily accessible only to the members of the particular religious groups who hold them, and as such they cannot provide the justification that is needed to support the enforcement of the basic requirements of morality with regard to gay and lesbian concerns as well as to any other issue involving enforcement.

Issues 4, 5, and 6

In addressing the issues of affirmative action, pornography, and sexual harassment, it is helpful that this book provides alternative moral approaches that lead to the same practical requirements, but that still leaves a lot to be done if we are to figure out what are appropriate moral resolutions of each of these issues.

For example, there are different kinds of affirmative action – outreach, remedial, and diversity – with different justifications, and even the harshest critics of affirmative action, like Carl Cohen,[3] don't reject all of them. So we have to learn more about the different forms of affirmative action and their proposed justifications before we can properly resolve this issue.

Similarly, there are different types of pornography. The distinction between hard-core and soft-core is widely recognized, but feminist critics of pornography also attempt to distinguish pornography from what they call "erotica," defined as "sexually explicit materials premised on equality," of which they approve.[4] So here again, these complexities will have to be taken into account, along with the resources of this book, before we can reach a morally defensible resolution of the issue.

There is also considerable disagreement concerning what constitutes sexual harassment. Consider the following. A woman complained about her workplace, where pictures of nude and scantily clad women abounded (including one, which hung on a wall for eight years, of a woman with a golf ball on her breasts and a man with his golf club standing over her and yelling "Fore!") and where a coworker, never disciplined despite repeated complaints, routinely referred to women as "whores," "cunts," "pussies," and "tits."[5] Was this sexual harassment? Most people, I believe, think that it was, but the U.S. court ruling in this case found it not a sufficiently hostile environment to constitute sexual harassment. So we would definitely need to consider a variety of relevant cases in order to determine what should be considered to be sexual harassment and how we should best prevent it.

Thus, with respect to the issues of affirmative action, pornography, and sexual harassment, this book does provide a useful moral framework for taking up the issues, but additional resources are clearly needed in

order to determine what ought to be done with respect
to each issue.

Issue 7

At first, addressing the issue of punishment in a society looks quite straightforward. All we need to do is
determine who is responsible for what crimes and then
determine what their punishment should be. Of course,
we would need to gather data on the crimes that are
committed in a society and the punishments that are
usually imposed. But having that, we could seemingly
determine the appropriateness of the punishment to the
crime.

Unfortunately, there is a serious problem with doing
this. It arises because many of the crimes that are committed in a society are property crimes where someone,
say Anna, takes something to which someone else,
say Pedro, has a legal property right. But what if the
distribution of property, which, of course, is virtually
equivalent to the distribution of income and wealth, is
unjust? Suppose, then, that what Anna takes from Pedro
is something to which she would be legally entitled in a
just society, but something to which she is not legally
entitled in the unjust society in which both she and
Pedro live.

How, then, could Anna be legitimately punished for
doing what she would be morally entitled to do in a just
society? It would seem that she could not. In this way,
we can see that at least for property crimes, the moral
justification for punishment in a society depends on
whether there is a moral justification for the distribution
of property (or the distribution of income and wealth) in
that society. The moral justification of the criminal justice system, at least with respect to property, depends on
the moral justification of the distributive justice system
that determines who has legal entitlement to property. If

the distributive justice system lacks moral justification, then so does the criminal justice system. Clearly, this is a useful and challenging way to approach the issue of punishment, relating it to the proper distribution of income and wealth, an issue with which this book does bring you quite close to a resolution.

Summing up

As this survey of the seven moral issues shows, this book does provide you with some very helpful suggestions for resolving these and other moral issues for yourself. That was its goal.

Yet perhaps you want more help. Well, it can be found by using *What is Ethics?* in conjunction with a moral issues reader that will provide you with additional data and arguments useful for resolving these and other practical issues. If you found *What is Ethics?* helpful, readings on moral issues will help you build on what you have learned by providing additional resources. Used together, this book and additional readings on particular issues should greatly increase your ability to resolve the moral issues we face in our times.

Notes

Chapter 1 Introduction

1 Herodotus, *The Histories*, trans. Aubrey de Sélincourt, rev. A. R. Burn (Harmondsworth, Middlesex: Penguin Books, 1972), 219–20.

2 Peter Freuchen, *Book of the Eskimos*, ed. Dagmar Freuchen (Cleveland: The World Publishing Co., 1961), 194–5.

3 See David Stannard, *American Holocaust* (New York: Oxford University Press, 1992) and Leonre Stiffarm with Phil Lance, Jr., "The Demography of Native North America," in *The State of Native America*, ed. Annette Jaimes (Boston: South End, 1992), 36.

4 See Benjamin Valentino, *Final Solutions* (Ithaca, NY: Cornell University Press, 2005).

5 Sometimes the thesis of moral relativism is objected to on the grounds that it is self-contradictory because although it claims that morality should be understood relativistically, the thesis itself is taken to be a nonrelativistic claim supposedly true at all times and places. Yet while the thesis of moral relativism does maintain the relativity of the truth of moral claims, the thesis itself is not understood to be a moral claim. Rather, it is understood to be a meta-claim about moral claims. For this reason, it does not follow that what the thesis claims is true of moral

claims is true of itself. Still, we might wonder why we should understand one class of claims relativistically but not another.

6 See Ernest Shackleton, *South* (Guilford, CT: The Lyons Press, 1998).

7 Deirdre Pirro, "Franca Viola," *The Florentine Issue* 78, April 30, 2008, http://www.theflorentine.net/lifestyle/2008/04/franca-viola/; John W. Cook, *Morality and Cultural Differences* (New York: Oxford University Press, 1999), 35.

8 William Dalrymple, *The Age of Kali: Indian Travels and Encounters* (London: Penguin, 1998), 126.

9 Patricia Ebrey, "Women in Traditional China," https://asiasociety.org/education/women-traditional-china.

10 Ibid.

11 From a 1989 interview with Aisha Abdel Majid, a Sudanese woman working as a teacher in the Middle East. Quoted in Rogaia Mustafa Abusharaf, "Unmasking Tradition," *The Sciences* (March/April 1998), 23.

12 http://humansexualitygroup4.weebly.com/gender-roles.html.

13 Of course, we could define morality so that it allows the interests of some to be basically ignored by its requirements. But this is not how we normally understand morality, and the "moral conflict" needed to support the thesis of moral relativism would simply be a consequence of using this unusual definition. Moreover, there is nothing to recommend this approach.

14 Dorothy Stein, "Women to Burn: Suttee as a Normative Institution," *Signs* 4, no. 2 (1978), 255–6.

15 Ibid.

16 The injustice of this Hindu reward and punishment scheme is quite evident. Right off, there is no comparable practice that obtains when wives die before husbands, as fairness would require.

17 WHO, "Female Genital Mutilation," https://www.who.int/news-room/fact-sheets/detail/female-genital-mutilation.

18 Frances Althaus, "Female Circumcision: Rite of Passage or Violation of Rights," *International Family Planning Perspectives* 23, no. 3 (September 1997), 4.

19 WHO, "Female Genital Mutilation."
20 Robert Darby and Steven Svohoda, "A Rose by Any Other Name? Rethinking the Similarities and Differences Between Male and Female Genital Cutting," *Medical Anthropology Quarterly* 21, no. 3 (2007), 301–23.
21 Althaus, "Female Circumcision," 2.
22 Since religious reasons are by definition not reasonably acceptable to everyone but only to members of particular religious faiths, it is important that such reasons not be used to support one's side in this debate, or in any other debate whose resolution will involve the use of governmental coercion. See Chapter 6 for further argument.

Chapter 2 Why be Moral?

1 Plato, *The Republic*, trans. G. M. A. Grube (Indianapolis: Hackett, 1974), Book II.
2 Ponzi schemes are named after Charles Ponzi, who became notorious for using the technique in the early 20th century.
3 David Voreacos and David Glovin, "Madoff Confessed $50 Billion Fraud Before FBI Arrest," *Bloomberg News*, December 13, 2008, http://www.bloomberg.com/apps/news?picl=newsarchive&sid=atUk.Qn.XAvZY.
4 Such an individual is imagined to be just another limited creature, like ourselves, not God, who is thought to be all good and all powerful.
5 James Rachels, as we shall see, confounds these two forms of egoism, taking an argument that works against Individual Ethical Egoism to also work against Universal Ethical Egoism, when it doesn't. See the discussion later in this text.
6 Christine Korsgaard, "The Sources of Normativity," *The Tanner Lectures on Human Values* (Salt Lake City: University of Utah Press, 1992), https://tanner lectures.utah.edu/_documents/a-to-z/k/korsgaard94. pdf. Although Korsgaard puts her publicity objection to egoism somewhat differently than I have here – she compares egoism to a private language – the egoist's response to both forms of the objection is the same.
7 It should be clear that both Gyges and Madoff are

committed to Universal Ethical Egoism, and not to Individual Ethical Egoism, because their behavior nowhere suggests that they are the only ones who should be acting egoistically.

8 James Rachels, *The Elements of Moral Philosophy*, 7th ed. (New York: McGraw-Hill, 2012), 77.

9 Rachels fails to distinguish between these two forms of egoism, blurring them together. This explains why he doesn't see that his argument against the one form of egoism does not work against the other.

10 Kurt Baier, *The Moral Point of View* (Ithaca, NY: Cornell University Press, 1958), 188–91.

11 Jesse Kahn, "In Defense of Egoism," in *Morality and Rational Self-Interest*, ed. David Gauthier (Englewood Cliffs, NJ: Prentice Hall, 1970), 73–4.

12 To claim, however, that the "oughts" in competitive games are analogous to the "oughts" of Universal Ethical Egoism does not mean there are no differences between them. Most importantly, competitive games are governed by moral constraints such that when everyone plays the game properly, there are acceptable moral limits as to what one can do. For example, in football, one cannot poison the opposing quarterback in order to win the game. By contrast, when everyone holds self-interested reasons to be supreme, the only limit to what one can do is the point beyond which one ceases to benefit. But this important difference between the "oughts" of Universal Ethical Egoism and the "oughts" found in publicly recognized activities like competitive games does not defeat the appropriateness of the analogy. That the "oughts" found in publicly recognized activities are always limited by various moral constraints (what else would get publicly recognized?) does not preclude their being a suggestive model for the unlimited action-guiding character of the "oughts" of Universal Ethical Egoism.

13 John Rawls is typical here, as is Thomas Nagel. See John Rawls, *A Theory of Justice* (Cambridge, MA: Harvard University Press, 1971), 136; Thomas Nagel, *The View from Nowhere* (New York: Oxford University Press, 1986), 200ff.

14 See, for example, Christine Korsgaard, *The Sources of*

Normativity (Cambridge: Cambridge University Press, 1996).

15 "Ought" presupposes "can" here. So unless people have the capacity to entertain and follow both self-interested and moral reasons for acting, it does not make any sense asking whether they ought or ought not to do so. Moreover, moral reasons here are understood to necessarily include (some) altruistic reasons but not necessarily exclude (all) self-interested reasons. So the question of whether it would be rational for us to follow self-interested reasons rather than moral reasons should be understood as the question of whether it would be rational for us to follow self-interested reasons exclusively rather than an appropriate set of self-interested reasons and altruistic reasons that can be taken to constitute the class of moral reasons.

16 The altruist is here understood to be the mirror image of the egoist. Whereas the egoist thinks that the interests of others count for them but not for herself, except instrumentally, the altruist thinks that her own interests count for others but not for herself, except instrumentally.

17 For a discussion of the causal links involved here, see *Marketing and Promotion of Infant Formula in Developing Countries: Hearings Before the Subcommittee on International Economic Policy and Trade of the Committee on Foreign Affairs, House of 1980* (Washington, DC: GPO, 1980). See also Maggie McComas, Geoffrey A. Fookes, and George Taucher, *The Dilemma of Third World Nutrition: Nestlé and the Role of Infant Formula* ([No place specified]: Nestlé S. A., 1983).

18 Assume that both jobs have the same beneficial effects on the interests of others.

19 This is because, as we shall see, morality itself already represents a compromise between egoism and altruism. So to ask that moral reasons be weighed against self-interested reasons is, in effect, to count self-interested reasons twice: once in the compromise between egoism and altruism and then again when moral reasons are weighed against self-interested reasons. But to count self-interested reasons twice is clearly to show a rationally inappropriate bias in favor of such reasons.

20 Assume that all these methods of waste disposal have roughly the same amount of beneficial effects on the interests of others.

21 Notice that by "egoistic perspective" here I mean the view that grants the prima facie relevance of both egoistic and altruistic reasons to rational choice and then tries to argue for the superiority of egoistic reasons. Similarly, by "altruistic perspective" I mean the view that grants the prima facie relevance of both egoistic and altruistic reasons to rational choice and then tries to argue for the superiority of altruistic reasons.

22 For further discussion, see James P. Sterba, "Completing the Kantian Project: From Rationality to Equality," Presidential Address to the APA, *Proceedings and Addresses of the American Philosophical Association* 82, no. 2 (November 2008), 47–83.

Chapter 3 Consequentialism

1 Jane Mayer, *The Dark Side* (New York: Doubleday, 2008), 9–10.

2 See Ruth Blakeley and Sam Raphael, "British Torture in the 'War on Terror,'" *European Journal of International Relations* 23, no. 2 (2017), 243–66.

3 In the few statements by U.S. officials claiming that the United States ruled out the use of torture against detainees, the text made it clear that the CIA, at least, was exempt from this prohibition. See Mayer, *The Dark Side*, 125.

4 Jeremy Bentham, *An Introduction to the Principles of Morals and Legislation* (Mineola, NY: Dover, 2007), 2.

5 John Stuart Mill, *Utilitarianism*, 2nd ed. (Indianapolis: Hackett, 2001), 17.

6 Bentham did, however, allow that pleasures could still be compared in terms of their intensity, duration, certainty, nearness, fruitfulness, and purity.

7 Mill, *Utilitarianism*, 10.

8 See Bybee Memo: http://www.tomjoad.org/bybeememo. htm.

9 Interestingly, the Bush lawyers claimed that even what constituted torture by their definition could be justified if the president authorized it.

10 The use of torture by the Bush administration initially provided evidence for a link between Saddam Hussein and al-Qaeda, but later that evidence was discredited. See Mayer, *The Dark Side*, Chapter 6.

11 Catherine Lutz, "Research Cites 225,000 Lives Lost and U.S. $4 Trillion in Spending on Post-9/11 Wars," Watson Institute, Brown University, June 28, 2011, https://watson.brown.edu/news/2011/research-cites-225000-lives-lost-and-us4-trillion-spending-post-911-wars. See also Daniel Trotta, "Iraq War Costs U.S. More Than $2 Trillion," Reuters, March 14, 2013, https://www.reuters.com/article/us-iraq-war-anniversary-idUSBRE92D0PG20130314, and Stewart Smith, "The Cost of War since September 11, 2001," The Balance: Careers, June 6, 2019, https://www.thebalancecareers.com/the-cost-of-war-3356924. British deaths and casualties were less than one-tenth of these totals.

12 We may still be required to pay or make up for damages caused by consequences of our actions that we could not have reasonably expected that we would cause and so are not morally blameworthy for causing. The justification for requiring this seems to be the idea that someone has to pay for the damages, and so why not have the person who causes them, even if accidentally, be the one to pay for them.

13 Unfortunately, both sides in these conflicts have appealed to religious justifications for what they were doing. However, since such justifications are at best only acceptable to the fellow members of particular religious groups, they provide no neutral way of pursuing a consequentialist justification. In Chapter 6, I argue that the only way to deal with this problem is to appeal only to nonreligiously based reasons when coercive solutions are needed.

Here I am just going to assume that the consequences that are being appealed in our discussion to support coercive action have a nonreligious justification that all sides can, in principle, appreciate.

14 See Philippa Foot, "The Problem of Abortion and the Doctrine of Double Effect," *Oxford Review* 5 (1967), 5–15.

15 In the United States and Canada, the recreational pastime

of exploring wild (generally non-commercial) cave sys-
tems is known as spelunking. In the United Kingdom and
Ireland, that pastime is known as potholing.

16 Mayer, *The Dark Side*, 104–6.

Chapter 4 Nonconsequentialism

1 Immanuel Kant, *Foundations of the Metaphysics of
Morals*, trans. Lewis Beck (Indianapolis: Bobbs-Merrill,
1959), 422.

2 Ibid., 423.

3 Ibid.

4 Ibid., 424.

5 Kant further contrasts morality with self-interest by
characterizing morality as unconditionally binding (independent of what we happen to desire). For example, our
obligation to keep our promises is usually understood to
be binding whether or not we desire to keep our promises.
But the same holds true of self-interest. What is really
in our self-interest, or really for our own good, is also
binding, independent of what we happen to desire. As
the majority of cigarette smokers can surely attest, what
is truly in their interest is often contrary to the persistent
desires they have to smoke. Accordingly, the requirements of morality cannot be claimed to be rationally
required over those of self-interest on the grounds that
they are unconditional (independent of what we happen
to desire), whereas the requirements of self-interest are
not.

6 Nor would the egoist accept the Kantian view that the
only thing good without qualification is a good will, that
is, a morally good will, unless Kant was successful in
showing that the Categorical Imperative is a requirement
of rationality, just what the egoist denies. Without such
an argument, the egoist would probably regard Kant's
good will as something that is in her interest that others
have, but not something that is in her interest that she
herself should have. That way the egoist would be able
to consistently take unfair advantage of others having a
good will.

7 Kant, *Foundations of the Metaphysics of Morals*, 430.

8 Aristotle, *Nicomachean Ethics*, trans. David Ross, rev.

J. L. Ackrill and J. O. Urmson (New York: Oxford University Press, 1980), 1103a33.

9 Notice this is similar to the way we conceived of Morality as Compromise in Chapter 2.

10 Alasdair MacIntyre, *After Virtue*, rev. ed. (Notre Dame, IN: University of Notre Dame Press, 1984), Chapter 14.

11 Martha Nussbaum, "Non-Relative Virtues: An Aristotelian Approach," in *Ethics: The Big Questions*, 2nd ed., ed. James P. Sterba (Oxford: Blackwell, 2009), 349–70.

12 See Julia Annas, "Ancient Ethics and Modern Ethics," in *Ethics: The Big Questions*, 2nd ed., ed. James P. Sterba (Oxford: Blackwell, 2009), 419–34; Robert Adams, *A Theory of Virtue* (Oxford: Oxford University Press, 2006), Chapter 5.

13 Walter Schaller, "Are Virtues No More than Dispositions to Obey Moral Rules?" *Philosophy* 20 (July 1990), 195–207.

14 Rosalind Hursthouse claims "that virtue ethics not only comes up with rules (. . . couched in terms derived from the virtues and vices) but, further, does not exclude the more familiar deontologists' rules." *On Virtue Ethics* (Oxford: Oxford University Press, 1999), 39. Rules of the first sort would be of the less informative kind we considered. Those of the second sort would be of the more informative kind we considered.

15 Rosalind Hursthouse, "Normative Virtue Ethics," in *Ethics: The Big Questions*, 2nd ed., ed. James P. Sterba (Oxford: Blackwell, 2009), 389–99.

16 Aristotle, *Nicomachean Ethics*, 2203a–b.

17 Ayn Rand, *The Virtue of Selfishness* (New York: New American Library, 1964), viii.

18 Ibid., 30.

19 Rand still retains gender roles within her self-interested ideal. See Ayn Rand, "About a Woman President," in *The Voice of Reason*, ed. Leonard Peikoff and Peter Schwartz (New York: New American Library, 1988), 267–70.

20 Ayn Rand, *The Fountainhead* (New York: Bobbs-Merrill, 1943), 684.

21 Rand, *The Virtue of Selfishness*, 54.

22 Ibid., 56.

Chapter 5 Reconciliation

1 Nor would it make sense to reject the reasonable constraints imposed by morality by the expanded "Ought" implies "Can" principle in favor of the maximization of utility, because that would place consequentialists outside of morality. This is because the "Ought" implies "Can" principle helps to specify what is a moral view.

2 John Rawls, *A Theory of Justice* (Cambridge, MA: Harvard University Press, 1971).

3 F. A. Hayek, *The Constitution of Liberty* (Chicago: University of Chicago Press, 1960), 11.

4 John Hospers, *Libertarianism* (Los Angeles: Nash Publishing, 1971), 5.

5 Robert Nozick, *Anarchy, State, and Utopia* (Oxford: Blackwell, 2003), 163.

6 Basic needs, if not satisfied, lead to significant lacks or deficiencies with respect to a standard of mental and physical well-being. Thus, a person's needs for food, shelter, medical care, protection, companionship, and self-development are, at least in part, needs of this sort. For a discussion of basic needs, see James P. Sterba, *How to Make People Just* (Lanham, MD: Rowman & Littlefield, 1988), 45–8.

7 Libertarians have never rejected the need for enforcement when important liberties are at stake.

8 Sterba, *How to Make People Just*, 26.

9 Consequentialist ethics is invariably given a welfare liberal interpretation.

10 While there are some nonmoral uses of the notion of virtue, the Aristotelian appeal to virtue is clearly an appeal to moral virtue and that clearly does not provide any nonmoral standard to help us determine what is morally right.

Chapter 6 Morality and Religion

1 Some atheists and agnostics maintain with Nietzsche (1844–1900) that if there is no God (i.e., if God is dead), everything is permitted. And with this conclusion, divine command theorists seemingly agree.

2 Gen. 22 (Confraternity-Douay translation, 1963).

3 William of Ockham, "On the Four Books of the

Sentences," from Book II, Chapter 19, quoted and translated by Janice Idziak, *Divine Command Morality* (New York: Edwin Mellon Press, 1979), 55–6.

4 Thomas Aquinas, *Summa Theologica*, 5 vols., trans. the Fathers of the English Dominican Province (New York: Benziger Brothers, 1947–8), First Part of the Second Part, Q96 A5 Reply to Obj. 2.

5 Stephen Evans, *Kierkegaard's Ethics of Love* (New York: Oxford University Press, 2004), 156.

6 John Rawls, *Political Liberalism* (New York: Columbia University Press, 1996), 226. Throughout this discussion, it will be assumed that all citizens are morally competent, that is, sufficiently capable of understanding and acting upon moral requirements.

7 Luke 10: 25–37.

8 The sense of "unreasonable" used here and normally throughout this book is moral, that is, to say that something is "unreasonable" is to say that it is "strongly opposed by moral reasons."

9 Letter of May 22, 1860, https://www.darwinproject. ac.uk/letter/DCP-LETT-2814.xml.

10 John Mackie, "Evil and Omnipotence," in *The Philosophy of Religion*, edited by Basil Mitchell (London: Oxford University Press, 1971), 92.

11 It is mainly for this achievement that Plantinga received the John Templeton Award in 2017.

12 Responding to Plantinga's argument, Mackie himself conceded "that the problem of evil does not, after all, show that the central doctrines of theism are logically inconsistent with one another." John Mackie, *The Miracle of Theism* (Oxford: Oxford University Press, 1982), 154.

13 There is also an important advantage to my approach. On Plantinga's view, the explanation of at least some moral evil in the world is the constraints on God's power, and these constraints come from the truth of counterfactuals of freedom. But there doesn't seem to be any further explanation for why these counterfactuals are true. (See Robert Adams, "Plantinga and the Problem of Evil," in *Alvin Plantinga*, edited by James Tomberlin and Peter Van Inwagen [Dordrecht: Reidel, 1985], 225–33.) On my account, the explanation for some moral evil in the world

is God's goodness, and we are helped in understanding how a good God would permit some moral evil by analogy with how good human beings would permit moral evil in comparable circumstances. In this way, it seems that we can have a more satisfying explanation of the compatibility of the existence of God with some moral evil.

14 Imagine you are certain that your friend will come back to you later after he gets over his temporary depression and profusely thanks you for not being fully honest with him in these circumstances.

15 Notice that while the human agents act as they do in these cases partly because of limitations of power, God's permissive acts are to achieve some good.

16 For further argument, see my book *Is a Good God Logically Possible?* (Basingstoke: Palgrave, 2019; paperback ed.).

Chapter 7 Conclusion

1 Of course, resources on the earth will presumably run out for some "last generation" of humans, but as long as previous generations have only used what they needed for a decent life, no complaint could be legitimately raised against those previous generations.

2 Perceived wrongs, as opposed to actual wrongs, could be remedied by showing that no actual wrong had been committed.

3 See Carl Cohen and James P. Sterba, *Affirmative Action and Racial Preference: A Debate* (Oxford: Oxford University Press, 2003).

4 Catharine A. MacKinnon, "Pornography, Civil Rights, and Speech," *Harvard Civil Liberties Law Review* 20, no. 1 (1985), 1–70.

5 *Christoforou v. Ryder Truck Rental*, 668 F. Supp. 294 (S.D.N.Y. 1987).

Selected Bibliography

Adams, Robert. *A Theory of Virtue*. Oxford: Oxford University Press, 2006.

Annas, Julia. "Ancient Ethics and Modern Ethics," in *Ethics: The Big Questions*, 2nd ed., ed. James P. Sterba. Oxford: Blackwell, 2009.

Aquinas, Thomas. *Summa Theologica*, 5 vols., trans. the Fathers of the English Dominican Province. New York: Benziger Brothers, 1947–8.

Aristotle. *Nicomachean. Ethics*, trans. David Ross, rev. J. L. Ackrill and J. O. Urmson. New York: Oxford University Press, 1980.

Baier, Kurt. *The Moral Point of View*. Ithaca, NY: Cornell University Press, 1958.

Evans, Stephen. *Kierkegaard's Ethics of Love*. New York: Oxford University Press, 2004.

Foot, Philippa. "The Problem of Abortion and the Doctrine of Double Effect," *Oxford Review* 5 (1967), 5–15.

Hayek, F. A. *The Constitution of Liberty*. Chicago: University of Chicago Press, 1960.

Hospers, John. *Libertarianism*. Los Angeles: Nash Publishing, 1971.

Kant, Immanuel. *Foundations of the Metaphysics of Morals*, trans. Lewis Beck. Indianapolis: Bobbs-Merrill, 1959.

Korsgaard, Christine. *The Sources of Normativity*. Cambridge: Cambridge University Press, 1996.

MacIntyre, Alasdair. *After Virtue*, rev. ed. Notre Dame, IN: University of Notre Dame Press, 1984.

Mackie, John. *The Miracle of Theism*. Oxford: Oxford University Press, 1982.

Mill, John Stuart. *Utilitarianism*, 2nd ed. Indianapolis: Hackett, 2001.

Nozick, Robert. *Anarchy, State, and Utopia*. Oxford: Blackwell, 2003.

Nussbaum, Martha. "Non-Relative Virtues: An Aristotelian Approach," in *Ethics: The Big Questions*, 2nd ed., ed. James P. Sterba. Oxford: Blackwell, 2009, 349–70.

Rawls, John. *A Theory of Justice*. Cambridge, MA: Harvard University Press, 1971.

Rawls, John. *Political Liberalism*. New York: Columbia University Press, 1996.

Sterba, James P. "Completing the Kantian Project: From Rationality to Equality," Presidential Address to the APA, *Proceedings and Addresses of the American Philosophical Association* 82, no. 2 (November 2008), 47–83.

Sterba, James P. *Is a Good God Logically Possible?* Basingstoke: Palgrave, 2019 (paperback ed.).